Secrets of the Beechworth Bakery

Keep on Cooking

Best Wishes

Tom O'Toole

Secrets of the Beechworth Bakery

The Beechworth Bakery Cookbook

Tom O'Toole

with Lowell Tarling and Mathew McLaurin

Publishing

First edition printed 2001.
Second edition printed 2004. Reprinted 2005.

Published by:

Bas Publishing
ABN 30 106 181 542
F16/171 Collins Street
Melbourne Vic. 3000

Tel: (03) 9650 3200
Fax: (03) 9650 5077

Web: www.baspublishing.com.au
Email: mail@baspublishing.com.au

The National Library of Australia Cataloguing-in-Publication entry:

O'Toole, Tom, 1952-.
    Secrets of the Beechworth Bakery.

    Includes index.
    ISBN 1 920910 27 1

    1. Beechworth Bakery. 2. Baking - Victoria - Beechworth.
    I. Tarling, Lowell, 1949-. II. McLaurin, Matthew. III.
    Beechworth Bakery. IV. Title.

641.815099455

Cover & page design by Selina Low
Cover photograph by Phillip Ashton

"Any cook should be able to run a country" Vladimir Lenin

e-mail

dear tom...

HI Tom,

Last month I was lucky enough to travel Australia again with my husband. We rented a car and drove to Beechworth. Of course we visited your bakery and had a FANTASTIC time there. Thanks a lot. I got your cookbook, which is great! I, even I, can now make an OZ style yummy fruit loaf. It was my first time to make bread without any help of a bread machine. I want to try Murray mud cakes, Beestings, Date Scones etc., they are all my favorites

Bye

Naomi Abe

Dear Tom,

Just wanting to let you know that I bought your new cookbook yesterday. I stumbled over it accidentally and scooped it off the shelf like I had discovered gold! I have visited your bakery many times. I am a commercial cook by trade and have a love of cooking, particularly baking. Best of luck to you and many thanks for a great book, which I will always treasure! You are truly inspirational. I guess it is like they say: "You can not discover new oceans, unless you lose sight of the shore!"

Michael & Lisa Gough

I have just finished reading through your recipe book and was inspired to send this email to you. I am currently in China where my husband is working for the next 12 months. I came armed with only one cookbook, yours. I enjoy baking and breadmaking at home and thought I would continue to do so here, trying out a few recipes from your book....Can't wait to try some fruit bread as the dried fruit here is quite good. I'll let you know how we go. Thanks for a very readable book with some great life principles. Keep baking those delicious goodies.

Su Shearer.

My parents recently visited your bakery and brought home your cookbook. I have to say that it is the best cookbook ever! I am a 20 year old mother of 4 year old and 16 month old daughters, and I have always loved to cook. The recipes in your book are quick and easy, and so nice!

Perfect for mothers.

THANK YOU SO MUCH!

Melissa Gibson

Hi,

What a fabulous book, clear, concise and practical. Good to see a cookbook that doesn't require expensive, exotic ingredients. Next time I'm down Albury way, will have to make a detour to visit the bakery.

Cheers

Bonnie Stevenson.

Dear Tom O'Toole and other Beechworth Bakery people,

Last week I bought the Beechworth Bakery cookbook. It's fabulous! I'm retired, and have become a dedicated home baker, and I have a great collection of bread books, but this is one of the most engaging and helpful I've ever bought. It's down to earth, clear and helpful, and greatly enriched by Tom's snippets of wisdom.

Congratulations!

Terry Quinn

Oven Temperature

Note: All temperatures in this book are
recorded in Centigrade.

contents

contents

thanks

Mathew McLaurin (Mat) joined us in December 1985 as an apprentice and since that time he has worked at the Beechworth Bakery, apart from a stint in Canada in 1994 followed by a short stint in Rutherglen. It is real easy for me to make 200 loaves of bread or a few hundred pies or slices, but not so easy to make one or two. Mathew McLaurin is one of my great bakers at the Beechworth Bakery. He made this book possible by breaking down our commercial recipes to make them user-friendly in your kitchen. Mathew made every one of these products in his home kitchen (with home kitchen equipment), so his family put on a bit of weight when he got to the chapters on cakes and slices.

To my wife Christine a special thanks in helping to make this book possible. After working long hours at the bakery she came home and had to put up with us reading, taping and writing on the kitchen table, on the dining room table, and sometimes in my study. However, her contribution does not end there, Christine also read the manuscript and persuaded us to cut out most of the embarrassing bits.

Mathew's long-suffering wife **Sharron** gave up many 'family weekends' so that Mathew could take over the kitchen and cook up a storm. Sharron can also write legibly, which is more than can be said for Mathew, and she came in handy helping him compile — and structure — the recipe formats.

Thanks to Michael Bell and Phillip Ashton who have created all the pictures for this book.

Thanks to all of my staff, especially **Dianne Forrest**, **Marty Matassoni** and **Glenn Sullivan** who actively contributed to this recipe book, especially in the early stages.

breadwinner

This isn't just another bloody recipe book. This is a philosophy of life.

The average man finds life very uninteresting. He is always waiting for something to happen to him instead of setting to work to make things happen. For one person who dreams of making £50,000, a hundred people dream of being left £50,000. A A Milne, the guy who wrote the Winnie-the-Pooh stories, said that.

I believe in the power of positive thinking. And to me, cooking is a positive experience.

Nothing can make me happier than having empty shelves after working in my bakery all day. Not because the money's in the till but because people have bought the product and they love it. If you want to see a cook upset, it's when they see a half-eaten product left on a plate.

If I find a half-eaten pie, I'll say to my staff, "They've only eaten half the pie! What's wrong?"

And they'll reply, "It was their bloody fourth pie, that's why!"

I believe that life is like a loaf of bread — you get out of it what you stick into the recipe.

Some people won't bother to read this introduction. They'll shoot straight to the recipes — because they're hungry.

They won't know that the real reason I wrote this book is because my favourite recipe is my recipe for life:

1. Clean up

Clean up your kitchen — spring-clean your mind.

2. Focus

Remember that winners have two characteristics — definite goals and burning desires — so visualise what you are going to make.

3. Do it

Mould, shape, create, chuck in the ingredients and bake it. That's life.

4. Enjoy your reward

Stick all your hard work in the oven of life and enjoy your piece of the pie.

5. Be grateful

When it's all over, have an attitude of gratitude; you'll not only enjoy your experiences as a cook, but you will also have a good life.

That's what cooking (and life) is all about.

...Hello. I'm Tom, the founder of the Australia's most famous bakery.

Beechworth Bakery

I have written this recipe book so that anyone who enjoys our food can have the Beechworth Bakery in their kitchen. We bake everything on the premises at the Beechworth Bakery. What you see is what you get. And we get people from all over Australia and overseas. We're always getting requests for our recipes.

So I've written this recipe book.

My first book, *Breadwinner* — the story of my life — has helped a lot of people in their work and in their lives. I want this, my second book, to help you in your kitchen. Here's my story:

I was born in 1952, in Tocumwal, a NSW border town on the Murray River. I learned nothing at school, not even the alphabet.

At 16, I became a baker's apprentice at Toc. After finishing my apprenticeship in 1972, I went to Arnhem Land for 15 months where I taught tribal Aborigines to bake bread. Wow. We had a great understanding. They didn't know the alphabet either.

After that I opened a bakery in Yarrawonga, Victoria, which was okay, but I had a lot to learn. Then, in 1974, I bought the Beechworth Bakery and lived above it. That was okay too; I sold it to two boxers in 1977. They hung their championship belts on the wall behind the cakes, and the customers were too scared to come inside. But that wasn't my problem because I was off to Augusta in Western Australia where I opened another bakery and that was great. I started to innovate.

I made heaps of money and heaps of mistakes. But mistakes are life; if I'm not making mistakes, I'm not really trying.

In 1984, I bought the Beechworth Bakery for the second time. But I wasn't happy. I didn't like what I saw when I looked in the mirror. Looking back at me was 'just a baker'.

Then — one day, when the sun was shining — I took a second look and I must have been thinking straight for a change, because this time I didn't see a 'justa'. What I saw was a fully fledged baker, who was proud to be one.

And when I started seeing a baker instead of a 'justa', I was all right.

Now I'm proud to be a baker, so proud that I'm sharing my best recipes with you.

Baking is my career.

I'm in there 100 per cent, boots 'n all.

Baking was my life; today, my bakery gives me a life.

And one of the pleasures of life is great-tasting food.

I love the industry I'm in.

I think it's exciting.

People ask me, 'How can it be exciting making meat pies every day?'

It's because you're giving people a lot of pleasure, that's why. I think a lot of people in the food game feel the same way.

Notice I said 'food game'. I would never describe myself as a 'foody' because I don't have the big vocabulary that foodies have.

I keep it simple.

I want it fresh.

I want it now.

And I want it to taste bloody beautiful.

Scratch

I started my apprenticeship when there were no premixes in country bakeries (although there probably were in the cities). Everything was 'scratch recipes' and I still try to keep everything 'scratch'. We don't use many premixes. We start with a bag of flour and — if it's to be — it's up to me. Well, my staff actually.

We start off with a bag of flour in the morning and a few other ingredients, and hopefully at the end of the day, the Beechworth Bakery has a till full of money.

Old Favourites

As you would expect, I started picking up recipes from very my first day as a baker. I've still kept lots from my apprenticeship days and — to get that authentic cooking — I also have a quite a few recipe books that are much older than that. Plus lots of modern ones.

As long as it tastes good, that's the criterion.

The old favourites are still favourites today. The Vienna Loaf is still a good seller. The Chocolate Eclair — I must admit it is a lot better quality now than in the 1970s — but it was popular then, and it's popular now. The meat pie — look at it; it was a winner when I started and it's probably an even bigger winner today. We sell more meat pies than ever. That's pretty incredible — despite cultural change and multiculturalism, the meat pie is still No 1!

What a turkey!

I've been a baker in four states — Northern Territory, Western Australia, New South Wales and Victoria. I must admit I didn't see much innovation 33 years ago.

My first boss, Frank Hammer — now he was an innovator. It was a different world. The bakeries were independent, not centralised like they are now. We had a wood-fired oven.

At Christmas, Frank cooked all the hams and the turkeys in the wood-fired oven as a favour to the locals. One time we were cooking a turkey for a wedding. Frank fell asleep and ended up burning it. There was not even a chicken shop in our town, but the wedding was on that evening, so Frank hopped in his car and headed to Shepparton to see if he could find a substitute. Shepparton was a fair drive in those days and he bought every chicken from every café along the way.

I couldn't understand it myself. There were plenty of cockatoos and I'm sure I'd seen a shotgun somewhere.

Usually though, things went right. We'd stretch bread dough over the pig or the turkey and then stick it in the oven (the dough was not for eating, but it kept all the juices in, because the turkey or the ham were well protected from the heat).

Innovation

All independent bakers pinch ideas from each other, yet we all retain our individuality.

Innovation came to me gradually. I got into it in Western Australia in the early '70s. What gave me the confidence was the time I spent in Arnhem Land early in my career. Just like everybody else, the tribal Aborigines loved fresh white bread — they wanted it fresh and they wanted it now. Sometimes though, we had to make do with what we could get. One time we were finding it very hard to get good steak for pies, so I had to improvise, using buffalo. The pies were dark, gamey and tough, but they did the job. Not the greatest pie, but faced with either buffalo or dingo, I think I made the best choice under the circumstances.

One 'trick' that has remained since my stay in Arnhem Land is my preference for dried yeast. Refrigerated yeast wasn't practical in the Northern Territory. I still prefer to use dried yeast today because I find it more user-friendly, especially in the home.

However, I never got into the Aboriginal bush tucker in Arnhem Land. I never served goanna pie — it was too hard. I used to give my Aboriginal friends my apple tins and I wanted them chop the goanna up, chuck in the pieces and cook it. Who could compete with that? It was too difficult to gather wattleseed, catch snake and trap bush turkeys. It was easier to bake fresh white loaves — which is what they wanted.

And that's it!

I try to make what the customer wants.

Tom's Special

Later in my baking career I moved to Augusta, four hours south of Perth. We were on the southern end of the line. (After me, the deep blue sea.)

All bakers invent things and pinch ideas, so I started to do a loaf we called the Tom's Special. Before I saw anyone else doing anything similar, I started rolling fresh onion, bacon and cheese into a French stick. It was very wet because there's a lot of moisture in the onion. And it was a pain in the bum to do, but we became quite famous for that loaf, and I thought to myself, it pays to do something bloody different. The locals appreciated it, so next I invented the Health Loaf — grains soaked overnight in apple juice — like muesli bread. Nowadays, we take these fancy loaves for granted, but bakers had an extremely limited range back then. Nothing I do is original. Nevertheless, we got into it!

We're still getting into it.

And then we started to do fresh cream apple sponges, and that was sort of innovative because it was 'fresh', and nobody else was using genuinely fresh cream.

Having pinched so many ideas from other people, I'm willing to share my recipes and techniques with anyone. I'm always out there searching for new products. A lot of pastrycooks put a lot of mystique into it, but I don't.

Have Fun

We once did a six-foot-long loaf of bread for the Beechworth Harvest Festival. It took a lot of baking, energy and laughter to put it all together. We baked it on many trays in our deck oven.

Our pro decorator, Dianne Forrest, made a 'Bread House' for our year 2000 Easter Parade. She made it out of focaccias and block loaves and it was the size of a garden shed. A lot of work went into making that very large piece of Art Deco.

And it's the same in the kitchen; it might take a bit of work to satisfy your spouse, but it's got to be fun if you want to entertain your kids and make them happy.

I was a single parent for a couple of years and whenever I cooked something I always wanted my kids to say, "Gee Dad, that was terrific", but the truth is I wasn't a great cook in the kitchen. I'm much better at making a hundred of something than just making one. I find it much easier in the bakehouse where my scales, my equipment and everything else are at my fingertips. In a bakehouse I'm never going to get halfway through some recipe only to find I haven't got the ingredients to finish the job.

One real secret of success in the kitchen is preparation. Make sure you've got the sultanas; make sure you've got the eggs; make sure you've got the cream; make sure you've got the milk; make sure you've got the utensils or, alternatively, at least make sure you've got something else that will be a substitute for what you haven't got. If you haven't got something, make sure you've got something that you can be adapted. Preparation, preparation, preparation is the secret. Good preparation makes the job so easy.

My Bakery

When I come into the Beechworth Bakery, I'm one of the team. When you read this recipe book please appreciate that a lot of my staff have helped me put this together — it's not just Tom O'Toole — so I shouldn't get too much of the credit. In the Beechworth Bakery, I'm one of 120, and I'm often the most useless one.

I'll be speaking all over Australia and overseas. They have me up on stage and they give me a big clap. Then I come home and my family is sure to put me back in my place. I've got to take the garbage out, feed the chooks and run the kids into town, so I have a very stable base.

For me to be back to earth, all I've got to do is be back in Beechworth.

You see, there's no real glamour in the kitchen. There might be a bit of glitz in the shop when the beautiful eclair hits the customer's plate, but a lot of behind-the-scenes work went into making that eclair. When the oven bell goes off, you can't think, 'Wait a sec, 'til I get this phone call'. You've got to get to that oven.

The ovens aren't gonna wait for you.

The other bakers aren't going to wait for you.

You're part of a team.

I love bakeries. With a rolling pin in my hand or a piping bag, mixing the cakes — I am at ease, I am at peace. I feel safe; I know what I'm doing. My comfort zone is in the bakehouse.

When people visit any country town in Australia they head straight for the bakery because most of us bakers make a great product. Most of the time the customers are guaranteed a fresh product. And that's the same at home; when you make it from scratch and your family eats it that night, it gives you a lot of satisfaction to serve something so fresh.

Baking is very satisfying. It's probably the only industry in the world in which the retailer

has full control of his or her destiny. We start with a bag of flour and a recipe. We adapt, we create, we innovate. We make all these products; we put them on the counters; we sell them and the money comes in. From go to whoa, we do everything ourselves and we have full control. No other industry is like that. Whether clothes shops, chemists or newsagents—every other industry buys their product in. They're told what to sell and how to sell it.

But independent bakers can make and sell what they like. There are not many businesses that can do that. Bakers are not told, "These are your winter lines, these are your summer items, and these are your new releases for Father's Day". Even fruit merchants are dependent on their suppliers for their product.

No one has that control of the manufacturing, but bakeries do.

It's a pretty incredible industry.

Don't Make Grumpy Food

The great chefs love their job. If you're cooking and you don't really enjoy doing it, it shows in the product because the love's not there. Nobody wants to eat grumpy food.

If you think, 'I'm baking my guts out for the next three bloody hours and I bet no one says thanks', you're already telling yourself to be resentful. There's no use getting uptight about the time you're going to spend baking the meal. Learn to love cooking; lots of people do.

Put on a CD and enjoy yourself.

Make it a family thing. Involve your kids in our style of baking. Give them some dough and say, "Right, kids, roll out the pizza", or "roll out the focaccias". This is exactly what we do when school kids visit our bakery.

Above all, cooking is never a selfish occupation; you're doing it for other people as well as for yourself.

You make a lot of people happy when you do a good job.

Life's A Recipe

Life is like a recipe — you've got to have it written down. If you want to have a bloody beautiful family meat pie — first get your focus right, then follow the recipe. Break down your goal to follow your dreams. You've got to start by going shopping — buy the vegies, get this, get that, have fun. If the food tastes miserable, that's usually because a miserable person has cooked it. So smile: if you're happy, tell your face.

When I'm in the kitchen I like to have my mind completely on the job. I give my entire focus to the task and I don't like talking to people unless I know the recipe off by heart. Until then I dislike interruptions. And that's it — the results depend on the energy you put in.

Mediocre thinking gets mediocre results, and positive thinking gets positive results. So you've got to think positive, you've got to say, "I can make this lemon pie , or, "This strudel is going to be something special".

Then get in there, boots 'n all.

Your focus will take you where you want to go, so get focused and stay focused.

Baking is my form of meditation. It's my kind of therapy — just like some people find with gardening.

Why reinvent the wheel when you've got a recipe book? If you've got a recipe book, use the bloody thing and adapt it any way you want.

At the Beechworth Bakery we get heaps of requests for recipes. Fortunately, we have a Customer Comments Box, which has helped me design this book as a response to customer needs.

So in this recipe book, I'm giving you everything you need to produce beautiful-tasting bakery food, as well little tips and useful pointers. I want to tell you the tricks of the trade in our industry. I want this recipe book to be user-friendly and simple. I want this book to deliver a wonderful product.

If you see it in our shop, I want you to be able to make it at home.

Regional Australian Cooking

If someone were to ask me, "Tom, what type of cooking is in this book?" I'd say, "Homemade rural Australia". There are a few 'exotics' thrown in here and there, and our Japanese, German, American and other overseas visitors rave about the product. Yet, it is basically regional Australian product, although there are exceptions because I travel a lot and bring recipes home. For example, Beestings are from Germany, now they are from Beechworth.

Surprisingly, the old Australian favourite is still the meat pie, as it has been ever since I can remember. However, you can't get them in America — apple pies and pumpkin pies yes, but not meat. Independent bakeries are disappearing throughout the world.

In Asian countries, many bakers are highly skilled in artisan work. They create very finely finished-off patisserie work in Thailand, in Singapore — wow — and in Paris, of course. In Paris, the packaging blows you away. They do things like wrap up one eclair and then tie a bow around it. Whoa!

In this book, as in this country, a lot of our recipes are English rather than American-based. I regularly attend American bakers' conventions, but we don't get a lot of product lines out of them because their tastes are very different to ours. American tastes seem very sugary to the Aussie palate, and there is also lots of fat in American product.

I want this to be a usable book that you can grab at any time and say, "Let's knock this up tonight", or, "We've got guests tomorrow night; let's bake something special and have a bit of fun with the kids".

My two sons, Peter and Matthew, get into the kitchen and make up cakes and pizzas. It's wonderful to see them get in there. I find cooking very gratifying, especially when someone else is doing it.

I love doing it too because...cooking makes a lot of people happy.

Working for two hours and seeing it vanish in 10 minutes is wonderful. It is one of the joys of being a cook, because everyone loves you for it. When someone says, "Wow, these pies are just out of this world", it gives you the biggest buzz ever.

But when the kids say, "Gee Dad, gee Mum, this is bloody orgasmic, it is bloody beautiful!", that's great — you go to bed singing.

Sometimes though you've got to be a bit of a masochist to be a cook, because you slave over a hot stove, then you've got to do all the washing up. And if the kids are in a hurry, they even forget to say thanks.

Scratch Recipes

I use the expression 'scratch' recipes a lot in this book. And scratch means doing everything 'from scratch' — it's the opposite of using pre-mixes. I stay away from them, and that's how I've written this book.

It's sad to see the independent baker disappearing in lots of countries, because it's a hard game. What we're seeing instead are highly centralised bakeries where everything is made elsewhere, shipped in and they just bake it off. Supermarkets are taking over the world, and they have their in-store bakeries, but most of their stuff is processed in factories, untouched by humans. Furthermore, they use additives to give it a long shelf life. There's no skill or individuality in this, which means there's no passion and no love. Because they're baking on-site, some bakers tell the customer they're using 'scratch' recipes, but that's not exactly true. It's all pre-weighed. And the egg's powdered.

I wouldn't use powdered eggs. We use fresh eggs.

Independent bakers have that passion and love, because they're making everything from scratch. Most small bakeries (Mum and Dad businesses, like our Beechworth Bakery) don't put in additives and preservatives. We don't put chemicals in to give it a week's shelf life. We have that fresh product, and it's the freshness that gets people in. If you've got that love of the product, and you've got it fresh, wow! Who can beat that? Who can compete against the freshest and the best?

Who can beat that good attitude when you want to make a beautiful-tasting fresh product?

Our flour is either steel-roll milled or stoneground flour. It's not bleached; we use all unbleached flour.

Most of us in rural Australia make our sausage rolls and meat pies from local meat, yet we forget to tell people, "Support your local baker, who's out there doing the right thing".

Most independent bakeries forget to tell people, "Come buy it off us. We don't have a big processing plant. We make it from scratch."

Pre-Mixes

You can certainly get a big range of pre-mixes at your supermarket. All pre-mixes are pretty good. They are designed to work, and to work well.

Even though I don't like them myself, pre-mixes have four advantages:

1. They save all the hassle of having all the different ingredients on hand.
2. Pre-mixes don't take any skill.
3. They are affordably priced.
4. There's no real effort; a pre-mix is so easy that anyone can beat it up and bake it.

The same applies with the bread pre-mixes; you can make any bread now. It's all: (1) do this, (2) do this, (3) do this, (4) tip it in, (5) add yeast, (6) add water, then (7) chuck it in the oven, and that's all you've got to do.

I would guess that 75 per cent of bakeries use pre-mixes. The flour mills supply them and most city bakers use them, whereas we don't.

Adopt and Adapt

Getting a recipe right takes a bit of hard work. Sometimes you've got to use your brain, but not too often.

I say to my people, "Give it seven goes before you give it away." Most people give up after the first or second attempt, because it's very hard to keep going after you've done it twice and failed. "I can't do it, can't do it...", they moan. But I say, "seven times" — knowing that most of us get it right before then. You've got to keep persevering and persevering. Most of the time, if it's not working, it is the little things that you're doing wrong. The little things are always the big things.

And improvise. Take risks. Things get invented by accident. Adopt and adapt. That's where my innovation came from: I would use what I had and I would keep cooking. That's what I want you to do with this book: take what you want and leave the rest. If you're cooking at home and if you haven't got a round tin, use an oval tin. After reading a recipe, some people think, "I can't make this because I haven't got a nine-inch sponge tin" and so they don't do it. Or, "I haven't got orange peel" — so what? They've got another type

of tin, haven't they? They mightn't have orange peel, but they have mixed peel. Adapt and use something else instead. Who knows, you might invent the next Aussie favourite!

Forget the orange peel if you haven't got it. Lots of my customers don't want any kind of peel in their hot cross buns, so don't put it in. Lots of people don't want peel in their Christmas puddings, so don't put it in. Yet the recipe says it's there.

I want these recipes to be flexible — "I haven't got the pineapple, but I've got dates". That's flexibility. You've got to have flexibility.

For example, in this book you will get the basics of how to make a good meat pie, and if you get those basics right, you can fill it with anything you like. You can put your favourite chop suey recipe into the pie cases, or your leftover stew. Or, if you're feeling adventurous, you can make a barramundi pie, if you want.

The sky's the limit, if your heart's in it.

How To Use These Recipes

Everybody loves food.

If you love food, you should love cooking it, as long as it's simple.

If it's too bloody hard, it's too bloody hard.

The guts of this book is a series of recipes. Read each one carefully, bearing in mind the following:

- **Get ready.** Give some thought to your pre-preparation. Think about the equipment, clear the surfaces you will need and also take an estimate of the time needed for weighing, measuring, chopping, dicing, grating and so on. Set yourself up so that you don't find yourself racing to catch up with the oven.

- **Write a list.** I write lists for everything I do, especially lists of goals. Cooking is about achieving a series of 'little' goals, so I recommend that you write a brief timetable of your tasks in order. Tick them off as you go. Your list will read something like this, (1) get ingredients, (2) weigh them, (3) pre-heat your oven ...and so on. If you follow my advice on this point, you will never make an avoidable mistake.

- **Ingredients.** You don't want to get halfway through and suddenly realise, "I haven't got this ingredient", so have a bit of a think about the ingredients before you start. Assemble them and make sure you've got them all. If you are to substitute something to suit your own taste, now is the time to think about that, then weigh them out meticulously. At this stage I like to visualise those ingredients as the final product.

- **Get started.** The secret of getting ahead is getting started. So put a CD on, kick everyone out of the kitchen, wave the knife around a bit — and start.

- **Get serious.** Follow the instructions carefully. I must admit these recipes have been difficult for us to write. We've had to break them down into homestyle to make them user-friendly. Matthew (Matt) McLaurin has individually tested each recipe and put a lot of thought into writing them down, which is why I'd like you to read the instructions thoughtfully — as a thank-you to Matt, as well as a blessing to yourself.

We Eat With Our Eyes

I want this recipe book usable. I want anyone who picks up this book to find it easy to follow the recipes and get a great-tasting product.

At times we want to keep all the mystique to ourselves so that we can dazzle them with our footwork, but there are no secrets in our place.

We all need to know what the end product is supposed to look like. We need to know how it's done visually.

We eat with our eyes. If it doesn't look good, no one will be game to try it. I'll eat pretty well anything that looks good, so long as someone is willing to pronounce it for me.

Lots of people buy beautiful recipe books and hope they can get their knowledge by sticking them on the shelf. Closed books never open the mind

Tom's Tip — Seasons

Remember: your handling of the dough will vary with the seasons because you will be working in a much hotter kitchen in Summer compared with Winter. Although the baking temperature won't vary, your preparation temperatures will, because you will be kneading hot dough in a 40° Summer and cold dough in a 12° Winter.

Ingredients: What they do

Biscuit/Cake Flour

There are quite a lot of different types of flour available. Most flour is steel-roller milled, but there is also stone ground, organic, unbleached, bleached, soya, rye, rice, corn, biscuit and cake flour. Cake flour is soft, it's not what we bakers call a 'strong' flour.

Most asked Q & As

What is it? And where can get it? What does it do?

	What is it?	What does it do?	Where do we get it?
Yeast	Yeast is a single celled organism, a fungi. It needs water, food and a warm environment.	The job yeast has to do is called fermentation, this makes a gas called carbon dioxide and in bread this makes it sponge like and gives lift.	Use dry yeast from your supermarket.
Gluten	This is wheat grain protein. When mixed with water it makes a rubbery structure.	Performs two roles in bread making: 1. It provides dough structure and strength. 2. It traps the gas from yeast.	This is also available from your supermarket.
Bread Improver	This is made of oxidising and reducing agents, emulsifiers and enzymes.	Improver is a yeast food and also helps in gluten maturing and improves softness, texture and may extend storage life.	This is also available from your supermarket.
Rice Flour	Flour from rice, ground down.	In dough it helps in making bread more crusty.	This is available from your supermarket.

baking equipment

Bakery equipment is similar to what it was 36 years ago when I started my apprenticeship. It hasn't changed much.

Nowadays, of course, we have fan-forced ovens that have impacted on baking immensely. Sure, it's pretty flash and it's got all this technology, but it's just a bloody oven. We also have computerised dough sheeters, which is just a rolling pin. The same applies to all baking equipment; it hasn't changed much for centuries — except that it's flasher and more convenient.

Although it's been around for a long time, the fridge is the most revolutionary piece of bakery equipment in the long history of baking — and who hasn't got one of those?

Our mixers, tins, utensils and chopping boards are what people have used for ages. I've seen a photo of an 1888 mixer and it was pretty much identical to some of today's mixers. Dough mixers virtually use the same system as they always did, although today, of course, they're a lot quicker.

The following is a list of the equipment you will need.

1. Work Area

You need a work area — but everyone's got a kitchen.

Of course, you need a kitchen bench — but you don't need lots of room. The less room, the less mess. You also need a sink. Any sink.

And most important of all, the oven...

2. Oven

For best results, you need an oven that is capable of getting the temperature exactly right. No two ovens are alike. Buy a reliable oven thermometer and test your oven temperature.

Fan-forced ovens are the best because the air is even. Otherwise, you've got to remember to keep moving the product around because there can be hot and cold spots. Most people have fan-forced ovens today. All products in this book are baked in an electric fan-forced oven.

3. Refrigerator

We don't use our fridges enough, yet you can hold your dough in the freezer. Take pizza bases, for example. Don't just do up one or two pizza bases; know that you will be having pizzas next week or you'll have friends over in a fortnight's time. Wrap the base dough up in plastic, chuck it in the freezer, bring it out when you need it, put your fillings on and bake it off. You can do this with most of the recipes I'm giving you.

Stick the batter in the fridge until the next day when Aunt Dolly calls. Pull it out in the afternoon, then bake it off so that it comes out of the oven precisely when Aunt Dolly is due to arrive.

At the bakery the weekends are our busiest times, so during the week we do a lot of the preparation. We make up the batters and a lot of the doughs and stick them in the freezer and pull them out when we need them. Instead of baking it off on Wednesday for Saturday, we bake it off on Saturday for Saturday and we've still got that WOW — that freshness!

4. Microwave Oven

These Beechworth Bakery recipes are designed for a conventional oven not for microwave cooking. The microwave oven is useful but not essential. Today, nearly every house has one and it's a real asset for warming the icing, melting the butter and the chocolate (so you can fold it through) and other similar tasks, but not to cook in. You only need the microwave oven every so often, just for 20-second bursts, to do handy little jobs quickly.

You can't use a microwave oven for 'real' cooking — for example, when it comes to cooking pies, they won't brown up in a microwave oven. You need a proper conventional oven. Likewise, your best loaf of bread comes out of a fan-forced or a wood-fired oven. Bread is not suited to microwaves. But for those 20-second jobs, it certainly saves warming things up in a frypan.

5. Breadmaker

People who are interested in making bread usually have a breadmaker.

You can prove your dough in it, take it out and make what you want with it. Or you can cook the whole thing in there — from pizza loaves to multigrain bread. Most people are interested in making something different out of their breadmaker, which is where you will find my recipe book useful — for example, you can't make focaccia rolls and hot cross buns in a breadmaker.

It is certainly not a creative way to cook, and after a while it becomes repetitious; however, a breadmaker makes it easy to get results.

6. Bamix

A Bamix is a handheld wizzo gadget. It is a wonderful utensil for grinding the nuts for a harvest loaf.

7. Trays and Tins

You will need trays and tins for cooking in. That is, muffin tins, trays for slices, baking tins, bread tins, high tins, lots of tins. They will determine the shape of your product.

Use the same tray for multiple tasks — for example, your biscuit trays can be used for focaccias, pizza as well as biscuits. You can make your party pies in your muffin tins. You can use large cakes tins for fruit pies and family meat pies. You can even use large cake tins for your bread; make a round loaf — so what?

You don't need to buy tins; the best size is what you've already got — according to Matthew, even an old baked bean tin will do the job when you're sitting around a campfire and you've got nothing else.

8. Measuring Equipment

The measuring equipment that you will need is as follows:

- Proper measuring cups (not any cups). You will need to measure a regulation full cup, half a cup, third of a cup and a quarter of a cup

- A jar for measuring liquids in litres

- Spoons sets — teaspoon and tablespoon sets are all measured to certain specific sizes and can be purchased in sets of five with a key ring around them

- Scales in 5 gram increments—digital is best

9. Other Useful Equipment

- A handheld blender

- Wooden spoons

- Bowls

- Sharp knives

- Piping bags and nozzle set

- A cutting board would also be pretty useful — so you don't risk marking your bench top

- Baker's paper or greaseproof paper

- Tea towels (for what comes last!)

Clean Up

I think doing the dishes is pretty important, yet it's a job none of us wants to do. I quite like doing the dishes, because it doesn't take a lot of brainpower.

Some days the most important job I'll do at the Beechworth Bakery is 'the dishes'. One of my staff members will say, "Tom, could you do the dishes?", which serves to remind me that a job isn't over until the place is clean enough to start the next task.

Tom's Tip — To Enjoy Cooking

You'll enjoy your cooking a lot better if you clean your preparation area as you go.

How to Melt Chocolate

Chocolate is best melted slow and not too hot, this will make it nice and smooth.

The best way is with a pot of hot water on the stove, then place chocolate in a bowl on top of the pot. Make sure hot water is not on base of bowl or boiling fast, but just slowly.

Keep all water out of the chocolate. If you like chocolate thin for dipping, add some vegetable oil, only mix in a teaspoon at a time, don't over do it or your chocolate will not set.

The microwave is also another way. This can be touch and go, a few seconds over and it's stuffed and also smells bad. So here it is — place chocolate in a bowl with one or two teaspoons of vegetable oil, mix to coat the chocolate in oil. Give 20 seconds in microwave at medium high and stir. VERY IMPORTANT to stir. As you get hot spots in the chocolate. Repeat every 20 seconds or 15 or 10 seconds depending on how much chocolate there is to melt.

Continental (Crusty Bread), Rustic Rolls, Tear & Share, Garlic Twists, Herb Bread, One Large Vienna Loaf, Large Pasta Dura Loaf, Pizza Bread, Focaccia Rolls, French Stick (Baguettes), Basic White Bread, Tiger Bread, Irish Soda Bread, Multigrain, Harvest Loaf, Scandinavian Bread, Orchard Loaf, Pumpkin Bread, Wholemeal, Health Loaf, Turkish Bread.

bread is very sexy

I find making bread very sexy. There is nothing more positive than bread. A well-fermented dough proving up is very sensual.

Bread delights us every day. It's such a big part of our lives, yet most of us don't even think about it.

Bread is special. It's simple and honest, very delicious and very earthy. It's been with us for a long time and there's still centuries left in it. How many other things have been and gone, while bread is still with us? After all, they say bakery is the second oldest profession.

Although there's nothing mysterious about making it, bread has a certain mystique. It's alive and very therapeutic to make. Of the five basic food groups, the healthiest category on the pyramid is bread and cereal.

When you really think about how versatile it is I don't reckon there is any other food like it. If you want a quick evening meal you can do gourmet toasted sandwiches. Sandwiches are the traditional lunch of all Aussie school kids.

You couldn't get a more value-for-money product than a loaf of bread at $2.20–$2.50. Furthermore, bread is so much healthier than potato crisps, fish and chips, or biscuits. A banana on fresh bread, wow! A jar of Aussie-Mite and a few tomatoes, and you'll feed a family for lunch. That's pretty incredible. A loaf of bread, a bit of devon sausage, avocado and tomato, and you've got a meal. Look at the miracle of the loaves and fishes — you can feed more than a family!

Who doesn't love bread? I'm hungry now talking about it. Who doesn't love a fresh loaf of bread with their favourite cheese?

Or with honey?

Or peanut butter?

Or toasted with melted cheese?

Or soaked in olive oil?

Or lightly soaked in milk and egg, and fried?

Because you can put any different fillings on it, you never get bored with bread.

It's just endless. It's exciting, I don't know how people can say baking can be boring.

I'm not through yet; you can also freeze it baked or unbaked. If you're living by yourself and you make a loaf, cut it into sections, plastic-wrap it, stick it in the freezer and you've got fresh bread every day. If you want to warm it up, put it in the microwave for few seconds and you've got beautiful warm bread again.

And there are so many different sorts of bread! There's white block, wholemeal, black, rye, light rye, beer bread, whole wheat, sour rye, four grain, six grain, cumin, carrot, herb, carrot and herb, high gluten, low gluten, Italian, onion, corn, olive, barley, soya, bran, Vienna, Provencale fourgasse, buttermilk, chestnut brioche, country style, walnut, pumpkin sourdough, sundried tomato, schlinkenbrot, pumpernickel, Killarney Irish oatmeal, flat, focaccia, matza, organic, fruit, sesame seed, linseed. And even green bread for St Patrick's Day.

To celebrate St Patrick's Day we do green bread for a week, because the school kids want green sandwiches. Green is not a colour you would normally want to eat — except in leafy vegetables — yet the kids love it.

When I was a boy in Tocumwal, we never wasted bread. We often used stale bread. Soaked in milk with a bit of egg beaten through, dropped in the fry pan and then flipped over — it's absolutely beautiful.

What do they give you when you go to church?

Bread ... (and wine).

History Of Bread

Bread enjoys the most interesting history of any food because it parallels the development of the human race. Baking was around in the Stone Age. The Egyptians milled flour and baked loaves and cakes, as well as a flat round roll not unlike our crumpets. The rich ate bread made from wheat, and the poor ate barley cakes or a sorghum flour product known as doora. In ancient Rome, those who were too poor to eat meat, ate wheat and barley products.

In Australia, the history of flour goes back to antiquity, with Aborigines having made theirs from mashed burrawong seeds, which they would then cook into griddle cakes.

Bread is timeless and universal.

How To Knead Dough

- Lightly flour your hands and work surface

- Place dough on prepared surface

- Take the far edge of the dough, fold it over to cover itself then, using the heel of your hand, push the dough down and away from yourself

- Give the dough a quarter turn and repeat the pulling, pushing, folding and turning motion for five minutes or so, until the dough is smooth and rubbery. If the dough becomes sticky, lightly flour the work surface again, and also your hands

This mixing method is important to form the gluten structure within the dough.

How To Prove Yeast Products

(Refer to this for the forthcoming recipes in this chapter and also for the chapter on Sweet Doughs)

The fermentation of bread is really important. The 'proving' is the rising of the dough.

To make a prover at home:

1. Clean your sink, put the plug in.

2. Place a bowl upside down in the bottom of the sink.

3. Fill the sink with hot water to just below the top of the bowl (so the bowl looks like an island).

4. Sit the container or tray holding the dough on top of the bowl (island).

5. Cover the sink with a towel to let the dough slowly prove until it reaches the three-quarter mark. The other quarter will 'kick' in the oven.

Tom's Tip — Keep On Mixing

Lots of people don't develop their dough enough when they're making bread. Always use strong flour, and mix your dough well. Most people under-develop their dough. We have added gluten to these receipes to make it stronger as most supermarket flour is all purpose.

Plaits

Anyone can do a three-strand plait; it's just the same as the little pigtails that girls wear. With three strands you can't go wrong. I must admit four to six strands are very difficult, but anyone can do three strands. If you're not sure, try it with a thick bit of string or something else first — one over, one under, and over again — it's very easy. Left over right over left. Then try it with dough.

Croutons

To make your own croutons is so easy. Get a couple of slices of bread, cut the crusts off, butter them very lightly, put them in the oven and dry them out until they become dry and crunchy cubes, and there's your croutons.

Add a bit of garlic butter if you like, or a bit of herb butter very lightly to the bread. Cook at very low temperature, then let it dry out.

To Make Grain Bread Mix

Here's how to make a basic grain bread mix, which can be used in Health Bread, Harvest Loaf, Multigrain, Scandinavian Bread, Orchard Loaf.

Preparation time: Bugger all time

Ingredients:

Cooking oats (porridge) — 2 cups

Rolled oats — 1 cup

Linseeds — $1/_2$ cup

Soy grits — $1/_2$ cup

Cracked wheat — $1/_2$ cup

Sunflower seeds — $1/_2$ cup

Method:

1.   Mix all ingredients together.

2.   Place in airtight container until you are ready to use it.

Tom's Special Loaf

Having lived with tribal Aborigines in Arnhem Land shortly before living in Western Australia, I wasn't looking at product in the same way as the people who had remained in country Victoria or who had become bakers in the city.

When we ran the bakery in Augusta, WA, it was a destination location, away from the other shops. So, to get the customers to go out of their way to come to us, I felt we needed something different — something they couldn't get at the supermarket and something nobody else made.

In 1974, nobody did bacon and cheese loaves, but we did. It was a bacon, cheese and fresh onion loaf and we named it 'Tom's Special'.

It is really hard to mould because the onion is really wet and slippery. However, the end result was just lovely. We have since made a change — instead of onion, we now use spring onion — so it hasn't got the moisture in it and it's easier to handle. We still do the same loaves, though nowadays we call them 'Savoury Rings', and these are a real winner.

We do it a lot fancier now than what I did 25 years ago.

Tom's Special is very easy to do. Start with a 500 gram bit of dough, flatten it out, put a few hundred grams of cheese, onion and bacon on it. Prove it, bake it and garnish it immediately it comes out of the oven. While the loaf is still hot, sprinkle it with grated cheese and parsley which melts on top of the loaf. Anyone can do these at home using a basic white dough.

Continental (Crusty Bread)

Rustic Rolls, Tear & Share, Garlic Twists, Herb Bread, Large Vienna, Pasta Dura, Pizza Bread, Focaccia Rolls, French Stick (Baguettes)

The secret of Continental is to get the base right, then you can add and make many things out of this basic recipe. You can do Pasta Dura, which we bake in a cool oven for two hours, compared to Continental which is in the oven for only 40 minutes.

The Pasta Dura is made in a cool oven, so it's got a thick crust with a soft centre. We prove the loaf slowly and we prove it dry — no steam. The aeration is very different to our Continental, which we put into a low-steamed area (at home you would keep it in a warm spot by simply covering it with a towel).

We could call our Continental Loaf 'Diet Bread' if we wanted to. We could call it the 'Slimmer's Loaf', because it is the most non-fattening bread that we make.

Out of this dough, we make our Focaccia Rolls which we flatten and do the indentations with our fingers, and then we put olive oil on top. Some of our rolls have olives on top or sundried dry tomato or herbs, garlic and cheese. You can put anything on top of them. The only things to limit you is the little bit between your ears — your imagination.

We also do a Pizza Loaf which is around 500 gram in weight. Flatten it out, again — olive oil, sauces, flavouring, lots of fresh vegetables, salami — wow, it's just magic. Here's the recipe for continental crusty loaves:

Ingredients:

Plain flour — 3 cups

Salt — 2 teaspoons

Improver — 1 teaspoon

Butter (soft) — 1 teaspoon

Rice flour — $\frac{1}{4}$ cup

Yeast (dry) — 3 teaspoons

Water (warm) — $1\frac{1}{2}$ cup

Method:

1. Dry mix flour, salt, improver, rice flour and yeast in a large bowl.

2. Add softened butter and warm water. Mix together to form a dough.

3. Turn out onto lightly floured table or board and knead for 3–5 minutes to form a smooth dough (see 'How to Knead Dough' on page 23).

4. Place into lightly floured bowl in a ball and place in prover to rest $\frac{1}{2}$ hour (see 'How To Prove Yeast Products' on page 24).

5. Remove from bowl and continue with desired variation.

This dough can sit in the fridge until you've got more time to mess around and then do up your Savoury Loaves.

Rustic Rolls

Makes 6 Large Rolls

Preparation time: 30 minutes

Baking time: 25–30 minutes

Follow Continental/Crusty Bread recipe steps 1–5

Ingredients:

Filling:

Tasty cheese (grated) — $\frac{2}{3}$ cup lightly packed

Onion (chopped fine) — $\frac{1}{2}$ cup

Bacon (diced) — $\frac{2}{3}$ cup

Pizza sauce or tomato paste — $\frac{1}{4}$ cup

Mixed herbs — $\frac{1}{2}$ teaspoon

Vegetable oil — 3 teaspoons

Method:

1. Pre heat oven to 200°C.

2. Mix filling in a bowl.

3. Roll dough out to 30cm X 30cm spread filling over and roll up to a log then chop, chop, chop, one way, and chop it again the other way.

4. Split the mix into 6 and place in a large greased muffin tin.

5. Prove for 20 minutes (see 'How To Prove Yeast Ptoducts' on page 24).

6. Bake at 180°C–200°C for 25–30 minutes.

Tear & Share

Our Tear & Share loaves are like what some other bakeries call a 'Pull-Apart®'. We flatten the dough out and we'll put in broccoli, fetta cheese, olives, sun dried tomato. We'll fold the dough over, then we chop, chop, chop one way, chop it again the other way, and then we drop it into a tin and let it prove up.

You can put in many different things — ham, cheese, peanut butter, pumpkin and peas. On top you can put sesame, nuts, even corn flakes. It's quite fun to make, like mud pies for kids — or for grown ups. When it comes out of the oven, you just rip pieces off and you eat it.

Our Continental is universal and adaptable; as long as you've got your base dough right, you can nearly do anything with it.

Preparation time: 1 hour

Pre-heat oven over 200°C

Method:

1. Place desired filling on dough and press in.

2. Roll into a log.

3. Spread a bit of olive oil over it.

4. Mince up log into 1 cm cubes, and do it roughly.

5. Place in greased bread tin.

6. Reprove dough in tin for $1/_2$ hour.

7. Bake in oven at 200°C for 20–25 minutes, depending on filling.

Garlic Twists

Follow Continental/Crusty Bread recipe, steps 1–5. This will make two Garlic Twists.

Method:

1. Cut dough in half. Flatten out each half to 25cm by 20cm.

2. Mix in a bowl: $1/_4$ cup butter (soft), 1 teaspoon of minced garlic, 1 teaspoon of mixed herbs.

3. Spread mixture over flattened dough, then roll each into a log.

4. Cut log lengthways then twist the two pieces together like a plait and place on greased oven tray. Repeat this process for second twist.

5. Place tray in prover, replace hot water and allow to sit for half an hour. (See 'How to Prove Yeast Products' on page 24).

6. Pre-heat oven to 200°C.

7. Bake at 200°C for 20 minutes.

Herb Bread

Follow Continental/Crusty Bread recipe, steps 1–5. This will make two Herb Breads.

Method:

1. Cut dough in half, flatten each half of the dough out into oval shape to approximately 25cm long. Press with fingertips to make small indentations all over the loaf.

2. Brush with olive oil and sprinkle mixed herbs on top.

3. Place on tray and reprove (see 'How To Prove Yeast Products' on page 24) for half an hour.

4. Pre-heat oven at 200°C.

5. Bake at 200°C for 20–25 minutes.

One Large Vienna Loaf

Follow the Continental/Crusty Bread recipe steps 1–5.

Method:

1. Flatten dough out to 30cm by 30cm. Fold from top $^2/_3$ the way down, back over dough. Then from left side fold $^2/_3$ over towards the right, then fold right side over to left side. Press down after each fold.

2. Dough should look like a wedge shape, thick at one end, thin at the other, Starting at the thickest end, roll up towards thin end. As you roll, press on sides to make a cigar shape.

3. Place on greased tray and reprove for $^1/_2$ hour. (See 'How To Prove Yeast Products' on page 24). Place 3 or 4 cut marks across top of loaf.

4. Pre–heat oven at 200°C.

5. Bake at 200°C for 30 minutes.

Large Pasta Dura Loaf

Follow the Continental/Crusty Bread recipe steps 1–3.

Method:

1. Place ball of dough into a lightly floured bowl and rest for 10 minutes.

2. After rested, flatten dough out to 30cm by 30cm.

3. Fold top part of the dough $2/_3$ of way down back over dough, then from the left side, fold $2/_3$ of dough over towards the right, then fold right side over to left side, making sure to press down after each fold, Dough should look like a wedge, thick at one end thin at the other.

4. Starting at the thickest end, roll up towards the thin end, nice and tight.

5. Place on a floured Baking tray with seam down. Flour top of dough and place tea towel on top and tuck in loosely as dough will get larger as it proves.

6. Place tray in a warm part of the kitchen and let prove for 1 hour.

7. Pre-heat oven to 140°C. When dough has proved to $2^1/_2$ times its size, (proving time may take more or less depending on room temperature) then very gently cut with a very sharp knife down lengthways 2cm deep so loaf spreads open as it cooks.

8. Cook for $1^1/_2$ hours, cook for more if you like crusty bread.

9. When you pick up loaf and tap on bottom it should sound like a drum. This is how you tell if it is baked.

Pizza Bread

Follow the Continental/Crusty Bread recipe steps 1–5. This will make two pizza breads.

Method:

1. Cut dough in half. Flatten each half out to oval shape. Approximately 25cm long. Press with fingertips to make small indentations all over.

2. Brush with olive oil.

3. Add choice of toppings, e.g. eggplant, capsicum, cheese, olives, salami, onions, tomato, mushrooms, etc.

4. Place on greased tray and reprove for 20 to 30 minutes.

5. Pre-heat oven at 200°C. Bake for 20 minutes.

Focaccia Rolls

Follow the Continental/Crusty Bread recipe steps 1–5. This amount of dough will make six rolls.

Method:

1. Divided dough into six pieces. Roll into balls — rest for five minutes.

2. Flatten out, pushing with fingertips, 10cm round.

3. Brush with olive oil adding topping — cheese, herbs, garlic butter or olives.

4. Place on greased oven tray and reprove for $\frac{1}{2}$ hour (see 'How To Prove Yeast Products' on page 24).

5. Pre-heat oven 200°C. Bake for 15-20 minutes.

French Stick (Baguettes)

You really should eat your French Stick as soon as you can. Today, with the tunnel under the English Channel, lots of French bakers make the French bread and take it across to England every day. And now that they're taking the flour into London quite a few places are doing traditional French bread.

I must admit French flour is very different to Australian flour. Everything always tastes better when you're in some exotic place — like Beechworth — and in Paris the French Stick tastes superb. You always remember good food.

Basic White Bread

The basic white is 'our daily bread'. It's a softer dough than the Continental and our No 1 seller, which it always has been for as long as I have been a baker and a baker's apprentice.

Nothing can stop you once you master the Basic White recipe. You just go on from there and do plaited loaves, knot rolls and French Sticks.

There are many ways to freshen up bread. As we've seen, the microwave is a good one — put a bit of milk in it and stick it in and it can come up just like today's bread. Technology has changed a lot of things, but I never sell yesterday's bread.

People say, "Tom, why don't you sell yesterday's bread?"

I say, "Because I haven't got a secondhand licence".

Baking time: 20–25 minutes

Oven temperature: 200°C

Ingredients:

Plain flour — 3$^1/_2$ cups

Salt — 2 teaspoons

Gluten — 1 teaspoon

Improver — 1 teaspoon

Yeast — 2 teaspoons

Butter (soft) — 2 teaspoons

Water (warmed to body temperature) — 1$^1/_2$ cups

Method:

1. Pre-heat oven to 200°C.

2. Mix together flour, salt, gluten, improver, yeast in large bowl then add soft butter and warm water and mix together to form a dough.

3. Turn out onto lightly floured table or board and knead to form a smooth dough 3–5 minutes. (See 'How To Knead Dough' on page 23)

4. Place into floured bowl and place in prover (see 'How To Prove Yeast Products' on page 24) for 20–30 minutes.

5. Remove from prover, press out to 20cm by 30cm.

6. Then fold from top down $^2/_3$, then fold left side over $^2/_3$, then fold right side over top. This should appear thick at one end and thin at the other, like a wedge. Roll up from the thickest to the thinnest.

7. Place in greased tin with seam down, and using a knife, cut loaf, $^1/_2$ cm deep lengthways (replacing hot water in prover) reprove for 30 minutes.

8. Place in oven for 20–25 minutes at 200°C.

Options:

Before placing loaf in tin for final prove, brush with water and roll loaf in rolled oats, poppy seeds, sesame seeds or a mixture.

Tiger Bread Recipe

Tiger Bread looks quite complicated, but it's very simple. The mix is oil and rice flour which is quite a claggy gluggy mixture. We coat a loaf and when it bakes off it's got a leopard-spotted pattern, which is why we call it Tiger Bread.

Tiger Mix (Topping)

Preparation time: 5 minutes

Ingredients:

Plain flour — 1 tablespoons

Rice flour — $\frac{1}{4}$ cup

Salt — $\frac{1}{4}$ teaspoon

Castor sugar — 2 teaspoons

Vegetable oil — 2 teaspoons

Water — $\frac{1}{4}$ cup + 1 tablespoon — more or less

Method:

1. Mix together to make a smooth paste.

2. Place bread dough in tin from white bread recipe, spread Tiger Mix evenly over top.

3. Prove and cook like white bread recipe.

Suggested Fillings for Savoury Breads:

*   Grated cheese, diced bacon and finely chopped spring onion

*   Grated cheese and diced onion

* $\frac{1}{4}$ cup of grated cheese, $\frac{1}{4}$ cup of diced bacon

*   Other suggestions: olives, capsicum, ham, salami, herbs, garlic, tomato, mustard, chilli — these work well with a little olive oil added

Savoury Rings

Method:

1. Pre-heat oven to 200°C.

2. Press out desired dough 20cm by 30cm.

3. Place desired filling on dough and press in.

4. Roll up like a log.

5. Cut log down centre lengthways, with a knife.

6. Twist two halves around each other (to look like a plait).

7. Join ends together to form a ring and place on greased oven tray.

8. Reprove in hot water for $1/_2$ hour (see 'How To Prove Yeast Products' on page 24).

9. Bake in oven at 200°C for 20–25 minutes depending on filling.

Savoury Cob Loaf

Method:

1. Press dough to 20–25cm round circle.

2. Place half of desired filling on top.

3. Press filling into dough.

4. Pull edges into centre. Fold up and press down firmly.

5. Place the rest of the filling on dough.

6. Fold up, pull edges into the centre, pressing down on the centre — mould into a ball.

7. Place onto greased tray, seam down.

8. Press out so ball is flat on top. Make 3–4 cuts across top.

9. Top with seeds or topping.

10. Reprove in hot water for $1/_2$ hour (see 'How To Prove Yeast Products' on page 24).

11. Bake in oven at 200°C for 20–30 minutes, depending on filling.

Irish Soda Bread

Irish Soda Bread is in between a bread and a scone, yeast-free and made with baking soda. It is similar to bush damper — though not the damper you buy in supermarkets today, which has yeast in it.

When you're in Ireland, Irish Soda Bread tastes absolutely superb. Because you're on holiday and relaxed, the bread adds to the flavour and the ambience of the area.

They don't call it Irish Soda Bread in Ireland. In fact, they don't call it anything. When I visited my relations, they just baked 'the bread'. It was fresh and beautiful and I was hooked.

You can cook Irish Soda Bread in your cast-iron damper dish. Drop in on the fire with the lid on the top. It's a quick bread because you're using baking powder or bicarb soda, so you don't have to wait around for it to prove. You just knock it up. You make it and you bake it. It's lovely toasted.

Preparation time: 15 minutes

Baking time: 50 minutes

Oven temperature: 160°C

Ingredients

Wholemeal flour — $2^2/_3$ cups

Plain flour — $2^1/_2$ cups

Salt — 1 teaspoon

Bicarb soda — 1 teaspoon

Milk (room temperature) — $2^3/_4$ cups

Melted butter — 1 tablespoon

Finely chopped parsley — 3 tablespoons

Method:

1. Pre-heat oven to 160°C.
2. Sift flours, salt and soda in large bowl.
3. Add parsley, melted butter and milk, then mix to form a dough.
4. Turn dough onto lightly floured board or bench and knead until dough is smooth.
5. Press into 20cm round shape. Place on greased oven tray.
6. Cut 1cm deep across top of the bread.
7. Brush with milk or dust with flour or sea salt and olive oil.
8. Bake at 160°C for 50 minutes.

Multigrain

Multigrain is 'multi' meaning many — barley, cracked wheat, cracked rye, linseed, sesame, sunflower seeds, pumpkin seeds, any seeds you like. Out of our basic multigrain dough you can do many different varieties, e.g. rolls, sticks, flat breads, pizza bases, herb pizza bases, etc.

Makes: 1 loaf

Preparation time: 1 hour

Baking time: 20–25 minutes

Temperature: 200°C

Ingredients:

Grain Mix — 1 cup (follow Grain Bread Mix Recipe)

Warm Apple Juice $1/_3$ cup

Soak together for 15 minutes.

Plain flour — $2^1/_4$ cups

Salt — $1^1/_2$ teaspoons

Gluten — 1 tablespoon

Improver — $1^1/_2$ teaspoons

Yeast — $2^1/_2$ teaspoons

Butter — $1^1/_2$ teaspoons

Hot water — $3/_4$ cup

Method:

1. Preheat oven to 200°C.

2. Mix together dry ingredients in a large bowl. Then add soft butter and warm water. Mix in grain mix with other ingredients to form a dough.

3. Turn out onto lightly floured table or board and knead (see 'How To Knead Dough' on page 23) to form a smooth dough for 3–5 minutes.

4. Then place into lightly floured bowl and place in prover (see 'How To Prove Yeast Products' on page 24) for 20 min to $1/_2$ hour.

5. Remove from prover. Press out to 25cm by 25cm.

6. Then fold from top down $^2/_3$, then fold left side $^2/_3$ over towards right, then right side over top to left. This should appear thick at one end and thin at the other, like a wedge shape. Roll up from the thickest (top) to the thinnest (bottom).

7. Place in greased tin, seam down and reprove for 30 minutes (replacing hot water in prover) or reprove until 2cm above top of tin.

8. Place in reheated oven and bake at 200°C for 20 to 25 minutes.

Tom's Tip — For Softer Dough, Soak Grain Overnight

Soak grain one day before or use hot liquid and soak for 15 minutes to get a softer loaf.

Harvest Loaf

We got into the Harvest Loaf because we hold a Harvest Festival in Beechworth every year, and we have done so since 1993. On the morning of the festival, I just started to chuck everything together and luckily enough the loaf turned out beautifully! We don't make it all the year round, but we do make it at the harvest time. To make your Harvest Loaf, first soak the grain in apple juice, then add fresh apple, hazelnuts and honey.

Preparation time: 1 hour

Baking time: 20–25 minutes

Oven temperature: 200°C — or a cooler oven to allow for the honey which would darken up in a hotter oven.

Ingredients:

Group 1

Honey — 2 tablespoons

Apple juice — $^1/_3$ cup

Grain mix — 1 cup (follow Grain Bread Mix Recipe)

Soak together for 15 minutes

Group 2

Plain flour — $2^1/_4$ cups

Salt — $1^1/_2$ teaspoons

Tom's Tip — Improvers

Today, you can get an improver so you don't have to go through the three-hour process, which we did during my apprenticeship. An improver is a yeast food powder that will help the yeast work. If you use this, you can pretty well make everything up straight away; you don't have to wait for all that fermentation.

Gluten — 1 tablespoon

Improver — 1$\frac{1}{2}$ teaspoons

Yeast — 2$\frac{1}{2}$ teaspoons

Flaked almonds — 2 tablespoons

Walnuts crushed — 2 tablespoons

Hazelnuts crushed — 1 tablespoon

Pecan nuts crushed — 1 tablespoon

Diced apple — $\frac{1}{4}$ cup

Sultanas — $\frac{1}{4}$ cup

Poppyseeds — 1 tablespoon

Sesame seeds — 1 tablespoon

Group 3

Butter — 1$\frac{1}{2}$ teaspoons

Water — $\frac{3}{4}$ cup

Method:

1. Pre-heat oven to 200°C.

2. Soak group 1.

3. Dry mix group 2.

4. Add group 3 to groups 1 and 2 in a large bowl and mix together to form a dough.

5. Turn out onto a lightly floured table or board and knead to form a smooth dough for 3–5 minutes.

6. Place into lightly floured bowl and place in prover (see 'How To Prove Yeast Products' page 24) for 20 minutes to $\frac{1}{2}$ hour.

7. Remove from prover, press out to 25cm by 25cm.

8. Fold from top down $^2/_3$, then fold left side $^2/_3$ over towards right, then right side over top to left. This should appear thick at one end and thin at the other, like a wedge shape. Roll from the thickest (top) to the thinnest (bottom).

9. Place in greased tin, seam down, and reprove for 30 minutes (replacing hot water in prover) or reprove until 2cm above top of tin.

10. Place in pre-heated oven and bake at 200°C for 20–30 minutes.

Scandinavian Bread

Our 'Scan' (Scandinavian Loaf) comes out of our basic Multigrain recipe. One difference is that whereas our Multigrain is a square-tinned loaf, the Scan is a high-tin loaf and of a different texture because it's able to rise. This makes the bread much more aerated and softer. High-tin bread is more of a 'open crumb' structure, which is a much different flavour.

To make one loaf

Preparation time: 1 hour

Baking time: 20–25 minutes

Oven temperature: 200°C

Ingredients:

Group 1

Apple juice — $^1/_3$ cup

Sesame seed oil — 2 teaspoons

Grain mix — 1 cup (follow Grain Bread Mix Recipe)

Soak together for 15 minutes

Group 2

Plain flour — $2^1/_4$ cups

Salt — $1^1/_2$ teaspoons

Gluten — 1 tablespoon

Improver — $1^1/_2$ teaspoons

Yeast — $2^1/_2$ teaspoons

Group 3

Butter — 1½ teaspoons

Water — ¾ cup

Method:

1. Pre-heat oven to 200°C.

2. Soak group 1.

3. Dry mix group 2.

4. Add group 3 to groups 1 and 2 in a large bowl and mix together to form a dough.

5. Turn out onto a lightly floured table or board and knead (see 'How To Knead Dough' page 23) to form a smooth dough for 3–5 minutes.

6. Place into lightly floured bowl and place in prover (see 'How To Prove Yeast Products' page 24) for 20 minutes to ½ hour.

7. Remove from prover, press out to 25cm by 25cm.

8. Fold from top down ⅔, then fold left side ⅔ over towards right, then right side over top to left. This should appear thick at one end and thin at the other, like a wedge shape. Roll from the thickest (top) to the thinnest (bottom).

9. Place in greased tin, seam down, and reprove for 30 minutes (replacing hot water in prover) or reprove until 2cm above top of tin.

10. Place in pre-heated oven and bake at 200°C for 20–25 minutes.

Orchard Loaf

We call it an Orchard Loaf because it's full of different kinds of fruit. Dried apricots, dried apples, dried figs, sultanas, currants, raisins or whatever fillings you fancy.

To make one loaf

Preparation time: 1 hour

Baking time: 20–25 minutes

Oven temperature: 200°C

Group 1

Grain mix — 1 cup

Apple juice — ⅓ cup

Honey — 2 tablespoons

Soak together for 15 minutes

Group 2

Plain flour — $2^1/_4$ cups

Salt — $1^1/_2$ teaspoons

Gluten — 1 tablespoon

Improver — $1^1/_2$ teaspoons

Yeast — $2^1/_2$ teaspoons

Diced fruit medley (supermarkets stock it) — 200g

Group 3

Butter — $1^1/_2$ teaspoons

Water — $^3/_4$ cup

Method:

1. Pre-heat oven to 200°C.

2. Soak group 1 for 15 minutes.

3. Dry mix group 2.

4. Combine groups 1, 2 and 3 together in a large bowl and mix to form a dough.

5. Turn out onto a lightly floured table or board and knead to form a smooth dough for 3–5 minutes. (See 'How To Knead' on page 23).

6. Place into a lightly floured bowl and place in prover (see 'How To Prove Yeast Products' on page 24) for 20 minutes to $^1/_2$ hour.

7. Remove from prover, press out to 25cm by 25cm.

8. Fold from top down $^2/_3$, then fold left side $^2/_3$ over towards right, then right side over top to left. This should appear thick at one end and thin at the other, like a wedge shape. Roll from the thickest (top) to the thinnest (bottom).

9. Place in greased tin, seam down and reprove for 30 minutes (replacing hot water in prover) or reprove until 2cm above top of tin.

10. Place in preheated oven and bake at 200°C for 20–25 minutes.

Pumpkin Bread

Our Pumpkin Bread is a soft-eating loaf. Again it's a high tin loaf, it's a very soft crumb. To do something different, we put a bit of fresh mashed pumpkin on the top and we also garnish it with a bit of pumpkin seed. It's a lovely loaf, very easy to do, but it is a separate dough.

Another advantage is that Pumpkin Bread keeps very well.

Preparation time: 1 hour

Baking time: 20–25 minutes

Oven temperature: 200°C

Group 1

Pumpkin (cooked and mashed) cooled — $^3/_4$ cup

Group 2

Wholemeal flour — 1 cup

Plain flour — 2 cups

Salt — 2 teaspoons

Improver — 1 teaspoon

Yeast — $1^1/_2$ teaspoons

Gluten — $2^1/_2$ teaspoons

Pumpkin seeds (optional) — 2 tablespoons

Nutmeg — 1 teaspoon

Group 3

Butter (soft) — 2 teaspoons

Water — $^1/_2$ cup (depending on how wet pumpkin is)

Group 4

Mashed pumpkin — $^1/_4$ cup (for topping)

Method:

1. Cook and mash pumpkin for group 1 and 4.

2. Dry mix group 2 in a large bowl.

3. Combine groups 1, 2 and 3 in a large bowl. Mix together to form dough.

4. Turn out on lightly floured bowl and knead for 3–5 minutes, (see 'How To Knead Dough' on page 23).

5. Place in lightly floured bowl and place in prover (see 'How To Prove Yeast Products' on page 24) and allow to rest for 15 minutes.

6. Remove from prover and place onto a lightly floured board/table and flatten out to 25cm by 25 cm. Fold from top $^2/_3$ down and press down, then from left $^2/_3$ across to right and press down. Then fold right side over top and push down.

7. This should now resemble a wedge shape. From top thick end, roll to thin end tightly.

8. Place in greased tin, seam down. Reprove with new hot water for 30 minutes.

9. Pre-heat oven at 200°C.

10. After final prove, gently, using sharp knife, cut lengthways down centre, not too deep ($^1/_2$ cm) and pipe a line of mashed pumpkin down centre (group 4).

11. Bake at 200°C for 20–25 minutes.

Black Bread

We don't do Black Bread at the Beechworth Bakery, mainly because we're very Australian. If we did it, we'd only be selling two or three loaves a day, so it's hardly worth it. The only Black Bread we do is when the apprentice stuffs up and burns the Wholemeal Loaf. And not even their own mother would buy that.

You can keep Black Bread for a week, whereas we chuck everything out at the end of each day on principle. Even our health loaves and our rye breads are sold on the day they have been baked. Some people reckon we're mad to do this, and we probably are because rye is actually better the next day. So is Black Bread.

But we choose not to sell it because we don't want to get mixed up. We don't want to get into a situation where we are left wondering, "Is this today's or yesterday's bread?"

So we don't do any of that.

Wholemeal

When I started my apprenticeship, 'wholemeal' was a simple white bread recipe with a bit of blackjack (burnt sugar) added — which accounts for the caramel colour — plus a scoop of bran. They called it 'brown bread' in those days. And they still do Brown Bread that way in England.

I always felt I was 'getting at them' a bit, the customers I mean. These people were buying wholemeal bread and I knew there was no bloody wholemeal flour in it whatsoever, so I started to do a real wholemeal loaf instead.

To make one large loaf

Preparation time: 1 hour

Baking time: 20–25 minutes

Oven temperature: 200°C

Wholemeal flour — $3^1/_2$ cups

Salt — 2 teaspoons

Gluten — 3 teaspoons

Improver — 1 teaspoon

Yeast — 2 teaspoons

Butter (soft) — 2 teaspoons

Water (warm) — $1^1/_2$ cups

Method:

1. Pre-heat oven at 200°C.

2. Mix together: flour, salt, gluten, improver, yeast in a large bowl, then add soft butter and warm water and mix together to form a dough.

3. Turn out onto lightly floured table or board and knead (see 'How To Knead Dough' on page 23) to form a smooth dough — 3–5 minutes.

4. Place into floured bowl and place in prover (see 'How To Prove Yeast Products' on page 24) for 20–30 minutes.

5. Remove from prover, press out to 20cm by 30cm.

6. Fold from top down $^2/_3$, then fold left side over $^2/_3$, then fold right side over top. This should appear thick at one end and thin at the other, like a wedge. Roll up from the thickest to the thinnest.

7. Place in greased tin, seam down. Cut loaf, $^{1}/_{2}$cm deep lengthways and reprove for 20 minutes (replacing hot water in prover) or reprove until 2cm above top of tin.

8. Place in oven for 20–25 minutes at 200°C.

Options

Before placing loaf in tin for final prove, brush with water and roll loaf in rolled oats, poppyseeds or sesame seeds.

Tom's Tip — Don't Use Old Flour

Flour does go off, so don't use flour that's been sitting in your cupboard for too long. A couple of months is too long.

Health Loaf

My second innovation came about in Western Australia. After the success of Tom's Special, I decided to try a Health Loaf with grains soaked overnight in apple juice. Nothing I say or do is original, and I pinched and adapted this idea from a recipe for Muesli Bread.

Makes one Health Loaf

Preparation time: 1 hour

Baking time: 25–30 minutes

Oven temperature: 190°C

Group 1

Grain mix (follow grain mix recipe) — $1^{1}/_{3}$ cup

Sunflower seeds — 1 tablespoon

Apple juice (warm) — $^{2}/_{3}$ cup

Group 2

Plain flour — $1^{1}/_{4}$ cups

Wholemeal flour — $1^{1}/_{4}$ cups

Rolled oats — $^{3}/_{4}$ cup

Salt — 2 teaspoons

Gluten — 2 teaspoons

Improver — 1 teaspoon

Yeast — 3 teaspoons

Group 3

Vegetable oil — 1 teaspoon

Apple juice (warm) — $1^1/_4$ cups

Method:

1. Preheat oven to 190°C.

2. Soak group 1 for 15 minutes.

3. Dry mix group 2 in a large bowl.

4. Add groups 1, 2 and 3 together in a large bowl. Mix to form dough.

5. Turn out onto lightly floured board and knead for 3–5 minutes. (See 'How To Knead' on page 23)

6. Place in lightly floured bowl and place in prover (see 'How To Prove Yeast Products' on page 24) and allow to rest for 20 minutes.

7. Remove from prover onto lightly floured board/table and flatten out 25cm by 25cm. Fold from top $^2/_3$ down, and push down — then from left $^2/_3$ across to right and press down. Then fold right side over top and push down.

8. This should now look like a wedge. From top thick end, roll to thin end tightly.

9. Place in greased tin, seam down. Reprove with new hot water 30–40 minutes or prove until 2cm above the top of the tin.

10. Bake in oven at 190°C for 25–20 minutes.

Tom's Tip — Quality First

To get a good quality product, use good quality ingredients.

Turkish Bread

Makes two

Preparation time: 20 minutes

Baking time: 12 to 15 minutes

Standing (resting) time: 1 hour

This is a sticky mix, you will need a mixer or food processor for this one.

Ingredients:

Plain flour — 3$^1/_2$ cups

Salt — 2 teaspoons

Yeast — 2 teaspoons

Warm water — 2$^1/_4$ cups

Gluten — 1 teaspoon

Method:

1. Pre-heat oven to 220°C.

2. Place all ingredients in mixer or food processor and mix for 10 minutes.

3. Cover bowl with plastic, wrap and let sit for one hour in warm kitchen, this mix will look like glue.

4. Pour half of the mixture very gently to make an oval shape on greased tray, sprinkle with rice flour or semolina, try not to knock to much as you will pop all the gas bubbles.

5. Brush very gently with milk.

6. Add toppings e.g; herbs, poppy seed, sesame seed, rock salt or traditionally a seed called Nigella.

7. Cook for 12 to 15 minutes at 220°C.

Tom's Tip

At home we cut the Turkish bread in half flat, add pizza toppings and grill in oven.

Cream Buns, Fruit Loaf, Apple Walnut Twist, Beesting, Valencia Loaf, Coffee Scrolls, Apple Scrolls, Apple Plaits, Hot Cross Buns, Boston Buns, Yeast Donuts

everyone loves sweet dough

Beechworth Bakery customers have always got a happy look when they're drinking a hot cuppa and munching away on a Coffee Scroll or a Beesting at morning and afternoon tea.

Everyone loves a Boston Bun, a Donut or a Cream Bun. A Toasted Raisin Loaf is probably one of the most in-demand breakfast treats around Australia. You don't even have to drive to Beechworth to get one; you can easily make it in your kitchen.

It's endless what you can do with sweet dough. You might do a cluster of buns and cover it with a bit of pink icing and pop a cherry on the top. You can do Elephant Feet or Bear Paws. They're just folded over with apple in the middle, and wow you've got Bear Paws. Again, if you get the basics right, you can't go wrong.

Most of our bun recipes, except for the Beestings, come from England and Ireland. We have adapted them to Australian tastes, and they're pretty authentically ours. Our customers' preferences are so established that we've been doing variations of the same recipes for 20 years, and they're still popular.

I remember when I was doing part of my apprenticeship in Albury, the sparrows would get into the factory and the first thing they went for was the Cream Buns. Just like the humans!

It's incredible. You start off with a bag of flour in the morning, and you're pulling scones out of it, you're pulling donuts out of it, you're making scrolls and Apple Walnut Twists, all out of this bag of flour — it's endless.

And you have full control of what's going into the product, whereas if you buy a pre-mix it might say 'Chemical 123' or 'Preservative XYZ' and you've got to look it up in a book to find out what the hell it is and whether or not it's poisonous. But by doing it from scratch, you know exactly what you're putting in — whether it's baking powder, soda, cinnamon, mixed spice, or maybe nutmeg.

Sweet dough is a little bit stickier. It's an enriched dough. It's got a high sugar and a high-fat content, which makes it very short eating, and very nice. We use sweet dough for our Coffee Scrolls, Apple Scrolls, Apple Plaits, Apple Walnut Twist, Boston Buns, etc. It is also the basic dough for our Fruit Loaf and our Beesting.

If you get the basic sweet dough right, the sky's the limit; you can make all those products — and more — out of this enriched dough.

Glazed Syrup

For Hot Cross Buns, Fruit Loaf, Coffee Scrolls, Apple Scrolls, Apple Walnut Twist

Preparation time: 10 minutes

Ingredients:

Castor sugar — $1/_2$ cup

Water — 2 tablespoons

All spice — $1/_2$ teaspoon

Method:

Place in saucepan on stove and stir until rolling boil. Paint on buns while hot.

Cream Buns

I don't think you can beat the good old-fashioned Cream Bun and it's so easy to do. It's a real easy treat at home. Sometimes we do Cream Buns without the fruit — just fresh cream, a bit of jam, dust them with icing sugar. It's so simple, yet what a winner. Just roll a Fruit Loaf into six round balls, prove and cook.

Fruit Loaf

Fruit Loaf is a real breakfast treat. Everybody with a sweet tooth loves it with jam, honey, Golden Syrup or — if you eat it warm — melted butter.

Makes one large Fruit Loaf

Preparation time: 1 hour

Baking time: 20–25 minutes

Oven temperature: 200°C

Ingredients:

Plain flour — $1^3/_4$ cup

Salt — 1 teaspoon

Improver — 1 teaspoon

Gluten — 1 teaspoon

Castor sugar — 3 teaspoons

Yeast — 3 teaspoons

All spice — $1/2$ teaspoon

Mixed spice — $1/2$ teaspoon

Nutmeg — $1/2$ teaspoon

Cinnamon — $1/2$ teaspoon

Butter (soft) — 3 teaspoons

Water (warm) — $3/4$ cup

Sultanas — $1/3$ cup

Currants — $1/3$ cup

Mixed peel (optional) — $1/4$ cup

Method:

1. Pre-heat oven at 200°C.

2. Mix dry ingredients in a large bowl (except fruit).

3. Add butter and warm water.

4. Mix to form a dough. Turn out onto lightly floured table or board. Knead (see 'How To Knead Dough', page 23) to form a smooth dough, adding in fruit, knead for 2 minutes, roll into a ball.

5. Place in lightly floured bowl and prove for 15 minutes to allow to rest (see 'How To Prove Yeast Products', page 24).

6. Remove from prover. Press out on lightly floured board 20cm by 20cm.

7. Fold from top down, $2/3$. Fold left side $2/3$ of the way over, then fold right side over top.

8. This should now resemble a wedge shape. Roll up from thickest to thinnest.

9. Place in greased loaf tin, seam down. Cut loaf $1/2$cm deep lengthways across top and reprove for 20–30 minutes (replacing hot water in prover).

10. Bake in oven at 200°C for 20–25 minutes.

11. Glaze with hot syrup (follow syrup recipe) while loaf is still hot.

Tom's Tip — Add Fruit In The Last Two Minutes

For recipes that require fruit. Add the fruit in the last two minutes, because if you put it in at the start, it gets mashed up, all the sugar is released and you can have a lot of trouble.

Apple Walnut Twist

Simon Bedbrook is one of my partners, and Apple Walnut Twist is his favourite. I reckon he eats the whole thing by himself in one sitting — they're that good.

Makes one

Preparation time: 1 hour

Baking time: 20–25 minutes

Oven temperature: 180°C

Prepare filling of:

Apple (diced) — $3/4$ cup

Walnut pieces — $1/2$ cup

Cinnamon — 1 teaspoon

Mix together.

Method:

1. Prepare Fruit Loaf recipe following steps 1–6.

2. Place filling on top, spread evenly over dough.

3. Roll into log shape, 20cm long.

4. Using scissors, snip from top of log down through log (not right through) every 2cm.

5. Lay semi-cut ring, one left, one right, one left, one right, etc. down the log.

6. Place on greased oven tray and reprove for half an hour, replacing hot water in prover.

7. Bake in oven at 180°C for 20–25 minutes.

8. When baked, glaze with hot bun glaze.

Beesting

Some of my customers are crazy. One wrote on my Customer Comments card, 'My brother reckons your Beestings are better than sex'— but he's only seven so don't worry about it.

The Beesting is one of our real signature lines. It originated as a traditional Germany recipe, and we Australianised it to the point that Beesting is now very traditional for Beechworth.

Preparation time: 45 minutes

Baking time: 20 minutes

Oven temperature: 200°C

Ingredients:

Plain flour — $1^3/_4$ cups

Salt — 1 teaspoon

Improver — 1 teaspoon

Gluten — 1 teaspoon

Castor sugar — 3 teaspoons

Yeast — $2^1/_2$ teaspoons

Water (warm) — $^3/_4$ cup

Butter (soft) — 3 teaspoons

Method:

1. Pre-heat oven at 200°C.

2. Mix dry ingredients together in a large bowl.

3. Add in soft butter and warm water and mix to form a dough.

4. Turn out onto lightly floured table or board and knead to form a smooth dough — 3–5 minutes. (See 'How To Knead' on page 23).

5. Place into lightly floured bowl and place in prover (see 'How To Prove Yeast Products' on page 24) for 20–30 minutes.

6. Remove from prover, press out with palm of hand into a circle the size of a flan tin.

7. Place in a 20cm greased flan tin and reprove for 20 minutes (replacing hot water in prover).

8. Prepare topping and filling, and allow to cool.

9. Once dough is proved in flan tin, gently place disk of topping on top of dough and place in oven and bake at 200°C for 20 minutes.

10. Allow to cool.

11. Cut in half, spread with apricot jam.

12. Pipe in filling. Replace top.

13. Dust with icing sugar.

Filling

- Prepare half of Vanilla Slice custard recipe following steps 4–6, allow to cool
- Fold 300ml of whipped cream through custard

Topping

Ingredients:

Honey — $1\frac{1}{2}$ tablespoons

Castor sugar — $\frac{1}{4}$ cup

Butter — $1\frac{1}{2}$ tablespoons

Flaked almonds — $\frac{1}{3}$ cup

Method:

1. Bring honey to boil.
2. Add castor sugar and butter until dissolved, stirring constantly. Do not burn.
3. Add flaked almonds after you have switched off the hotplate.
4. Spread topping onto greased tray in a 20cm round disk. Allow to cool.

Valencia Loaf

The Valencia is a beautiful, citrus-tasting loaf, and it's special. The dough is very similar to our basic dough, but it has orange and sultanas in it. Like our Orchard Loaf, the Valencia is lovely with an after-dinner platter of cheese or dried fruit.

My friend Gary Hudak in Mildura invented the Valencia Loaf. He's in the Sunraysia District of north-western Victoria where there are lots of oranges, which gave him the idea.

Makes one loaf

Preparation time: 1 hour

Baking time: 20–25 minutes

Oven temperature: 200°C

Ingredients:

Group 1

Plain flour — $3\frac{1}{2}$ cups

Salt — 2 teaspoons

Improver — 2 teaspoons

Gluten — 2 teaspoons

Castor sugar — $1^1/_2$ tablespoons

Cinnamon — $^1/_2$ teaspoon

Yeast — $1^1/_2$ tablespoons

Group 2

Butter (soft) — $1^1/_2$ tablespoons

Orange juice (warm)— 1 cup

Water (warm) — $^1/_2$ cup

Group 3

Orange rind (fine grated) — $^1/_2$ cup

Mixed peel — $^2/_3$ cup

Dried apricots (chopped) — $^1/_2$ cup

Sultana — $^1/_2$ cup

Currants — $^1/_2$ cup

Method:

1. Weigh all groups up.

2. Dry mix all ingredients from group 1 in a bowl.

3. Add group 2 and mix to form a dough.

4. Turn dough out onto lightly floured table or board. Knead 3–5 minutes to form a smooth dough. (See 'How To Knead' on page 23).

5. Add group 3 and knead into dough 'til evenly mixed.

6. Place in lightly floured bowl and prove for 15–20 minutes to allow to rest. (See 'How To Prove Yeast Products' on page 24).

7. Remove from prover. Press out on lightly floured board 20cm by 20cm.

8. Fold top down $^2/_3$. Fold left side $^2/_3$ of the way over, then fold right side over top.

9. This should now resemble a wedge shape. Roll up from thickest to thinnest.

10. Place in greased loaf tin, seam down, and reprove for 20–30 minutes.

11. Pre-heat oven. Bake at 200°C for 20–25 minutes.

12. Glaze with syrup (follow Glazed Syrup recipe — without spice) while loaf is still hot.

Scrolls — (Coffee Scrolls, Apple Scrolls)

The Coffee Scroll is probably the most in-demand product of its type sold around Australia. However, a Coffee Scroll is not what it seems. It is 'something you enjoy with your coffee', not 'a scroll with coffee in it'. There's no coffee in it at all, just cinnamon and spice. If you want that coffee taste, add coffee essence to the recipe.

Use whatever is in the fridge or the cupboards and a dash of creativity. Sometimes we make a slurry with cake crumb, jam, cinnamon, spice and water.

Other times put in castor sugar and sprinkle the cinnamon on the outside.

Yet another way is to smear a lot of margarine over it and then chuck a lot of cinnamon and sugar on, and roll it up.

You can also make Apple Scrolls with raspberry jam or with apple, or apple and custard.

Tom's Tip — Prevent Drying

Place cut scroll flat side down close together on greased oven tray or in cake tin (as this prevents drying out when cooking).

Makes six

Preparation time: 15 minutes

Baking time: 20–25 minutes

Oven temperature: 180°C

Follow Fruit Loaf recipe, steps 1–6.

Prepare Coffee Scroll filling or apple fillings, or use suggested fillings to preference.

Ingredients:

Coffee Scroll filling

Biscuit crumb — $^1/_2$ cup

Cinnamon — 1 teaspoon

Jam — 1 tablespoon

Water (warm) — $^1/_3$ cup

Instant coffee — 2 teaspoons

Mix together

Apple Scroll filling

Pie apple — $^3/_4$ cup

Mixed spice — 1 teaspoon

Mix together

These are suggested fillings; you may prefer to add blueberries, pecan nuts, walnuts, etc.

Method:

1. Pre-heat oven at 180°C.

2. Roll out dough, 30cm by 20cm.

3. Spread mix on top and roll into a log.

4. Cut 5cm pieces off log to make 6 scrolls.

5. Place onto greased oven tray or greased cake tin.

6. Reprove for $^1/_2$ hour, replacing hot water in prover.

7. Bake in oven at 180°C for 20–25 minutes, depending on filling.

8. Glaze with bun glaze (see Glazed Syrup recipe, towards the start of this chapter).

Apple Plait

I love Apple Plait. But if you don't like apples, put in something you do like — apricot, plum or whatever fruit is in season.

Preparation time: 1 hour

Prepare Fruit Loaf following steps 1–6

Filling

Tinned pie apple — $1^1/_4$ cups

Mixed spice — $^1/_2$ teaspoon

Method:

1. Mix apple and spice together for filling.

2. Pipe line of filling down the centre of flattened dough (20cm x 20cm), using all of the filling.

3.   Make four cuts from filling out to edge of dough every 4cm down both sides of filling.

4.   Take the left hand strip and fold it over filling to second strip on right hand side, and tuck beside filling. Take top right hand strip and fold over filling to second left hand strip and tuck beside.

5.   Repeat this process from side to side, folding and tucking, folding the last strip under the bun to hold it together. This should resemble a plait.

6.   Place on greased tray. Prove for 30 minutes. (See 'How To Prove Yeast Products' on page 24).

7.   Pre-heat oven to 200°C while proving dough.

8.   Bake in oven at 200°C for 20–25 minutes.

9.   When finished baking, glaze with 'bun glaze' — (see Glazed Syrup recipe, towards the start of this chapter).

Hot Cross Buns

I love Hot Cross Buns just with butter. I don't add jam or anything else.

I remember doing Hot Cross Bun doughs years ago when I was just starting my apprenticeship. My boss was a bit tight and we didn't put a white cross on the buns (although a lot of other bakers didn't either, I must admit). We just gently cut the cross on with a razor blade and my job was doing those cuts. I find it pretty hard today to believe that in those days, we cut everything with a razor blade

Anyway, I cut into all these fully proven Hot Cross Buns. I thought I'd done a great job in putting a cross into every one of them, but unfortunately I knocked the gas out of the whole batch — and there were trays and trays and trays of them, ready for Easter. My boss was ready to kill me.

I ran for my life.

I'd cut them too hard. You've got to cut gentle-gentle, and I didn't know that. See — with most breads and sweet doughs, you're selling air. It's a gas that rises. So really, to avoid all that hassle, I recommend that you pipe on the white cross with a piping bag — and away you go.

Makes six Hot Cross Buns

Preparation time: 1 hour

Baking time: 20 minutes

Oven temperature: 190°C

Ingredients:

Plain flour — 1³/₄ cups

Salt — 1 teaspoon

Improver — 1 teaspoon

Gluten — 1 teaspoon

Castor sugar — 3 teaspoons

Yeast — 3 teaspoons

All spice — 1 teaspoon

Mixed spice — 1 teaspoon

Nutmeg — ¹/₂ teaspoon

Cinnamon — ¹/₂ teaspoon

Butter — 3 teaspoons

Warm water — ³/₄ cup

Sultanas — ¹/₃ cup

Currants — ¹/₃ cup

Mixed peel (optional) — ¹/₄ cup

Hot X Buns — Cross Mix

Ingredients:

Cornflour — ¹/₂ cup

Castor sugar —2 tablespoons

Plain flour —1 tablespoon

Water — 3 to 4 tablespoons

Method:

1. Mix together to form a stiff paste.

2. Pipe on top of buns just before going into oven.

Method:

1.   Pre-heat oven at 190°C.

2. Mix dry ingredient in large bowl (except fruit).

3. Add butter and warm water.

4. Mix to form a dough, turn out onto lightly floured table or board, knead to form a smooth dough — 3–5 minutes.

5. Place in lightly floured bowl and rest for 15 minutes.

6. Remove from bowl and press out on lightly floured board. Adding fruit, knead together for 3 minutes or until fruit is mixed in.

7. Allow to rest for 10 minutes.

8. Divide into 6 even pieces. Roll into balls and place onto greased oven tray. Allow room for them to double in size (prove for $1/_2$ hour). See 'How To Prove Yeast Products' on page 24.

9. Make up cross mix following method. Pipe on top of buns with 1cm piping tube.

10. Bake in oven for 20 minutes at 190°C.

11. Remove from oven and glaze using Glazing Syrup recipe for buns.

Boston Buns

A buttered Boston Bun is a real treat for anyone. Here's the recipe:

*   Prepare Fruit Loaf recipe, following steps 1–5.

*   After this turn ball of dough out of bowl and flatten with palm of hand to suit size of cake tin, e.g. 20cm round tin.

*   Reprove for 30 minutes or until dough has doubled in size.

*   Bake in oven at 200°C for 18–25 minutes.

*   Turn out of tin and allow to cool on wire.

Boston Bun Icing

Icing sugar — 2 cups

Margarine — $1/_2$ cup

Vanilla essence — 1 tablespoon

Coconut — $1/_3$ cup (topping)

Method:

1. Beat margarine, icing sugar and vanilla together until light and fluffy.

2. Spread on top of cool/cold bun.

3. Sprinkle coconut on top of bun.

Yeast Donuts

You can't beat eating a beautiful fresh yeast donut, especially warm. Another good way is to enjoy them filled with fresh cream or even banana custard.

Makes eight donuts

Preparation time: 45 minutes

Baking time: 5 minutes

Ingredients:

Plain flour — $1^3/_4$ cups

Salt — 1 teaspoon

Improver — 1 teaspoon

Gluten — 1 teaspoon

Castor sugar — 3 teaspoons

Yeast — $2^1/_2$ teaspoons

Water (warm) — $^3/_4$ cup

Butter (soft) — 3 teaspoons

Method:

1. Mix dry ingredients in a large bowl.

2. Add soft butter and warm water and mix to form a dough.

3. Turn out onto lightly floured table or board and knead to form a smooth dough (see 'How To Knead' on page 23)— 3–5 minutes.

4. Place into lightly floured bowl and place in prover (see 'How To Prove Yeast Products' on page 24) for 15–20 minutes.

5. Remove from prover, divide dough into 8 even pieces. Mould into balls or roll into logs, 10cm long.

6. Place on lightly greased tray and reprove for half an hour.

7. Pre-heat deep fryer or large saucepan with 6cm depth of oil or fat.

8. Gently place spatula or pallet knife under Donut and place in deep fryer gently, flat side up.

9. Turn after 30 seconds. Do not overcrowd deep fryer. Cook each side for 2 minutes, until golden brown.

10. Lift out with slotted spoon and drain on absorbent paper.

11. Allow to cool.

12. Add jam cream, dust with icing sugar or roll in cinnamon sugar.

13. Cut long Donuts down centre and fill with whipped cream. Dust with icing sugar. Place fruit or jam on top.

14. Round Donuts can be rolled in castor sugar and have a hole placed in them and filled with jam.

Basic Pie Base, Plain Steak Pie, Gourmet Curry Pie, Steak Pie with mushroom, onion or potato, Steak & Kidney, Ned Kelly Pie, Pizza Pie, Chicken Pie, Caribbean Chicken Pie, Steak & Black Pepper Pie, Roast Vegie Quiche, Vegetable Medley Pie, Spinach Fetta Rolls, Quiche Lorraine, Meat Pasties, Bushman Pasties, Sausage Rolls.

You do not see the range of pies anywhere in the world that you get in Australia — except in New Zealand. They're not in Japan, Portugal, or America — which has Hot Dogs, pretzels and wraps instead. But in Australia, the Meat Pie is our food icon. I have even noticed it on the cover of Vogue magazine.

Pies appeal to people's imagination. For example, Elton John — who I'd expect to use a London-based cathedral — got married at Harry's Café de Wheels a pie shop in Sydney. Plus there are lots of poems and songs written about pies, like the Flying Pieman stories. Even in films, you'll see a Meat Pie with a metal file among the ingredients, made for someone in prison. First they eat the pie, then they file their way out.

We once held a Lemon Meringue Pie Contest in which contestants had to eat with their hands tied behind their backs. There was a bit of a panic when the radio announcer from 2AY Albury said, "Hang on, one of the contestants has lost his teeth...". It was a local guy who used to run the tyre repair shop. One of my staff had accidentally thrown his false teeth in the bin, while cleaning up.

Another time we held a Meat Pie Eating Competition at the Beechworth Bakery. The winner was a Kiwi guy from Albury. He ate eight full-sized pies in five minutes. He then went on to fame on television. He's a big boy.

He went on The Footy Show and became the state winner. He just kept travelling around the bakeries and he kept winning.

Times have changed, but not much. The meat pie is still tops; if anything, it is more popular than ever. A sandwich is a wonderful meal, but a meat pie is a meal-and-a-half! You can feed a grown man two meat pies and he'll be more than satisfied.

However, if you don't have good pastry, the pie will disintegrate, so it's pretty important that you have a good casing — as well as a good filling. (If you can do a good stew, you can do a good filling.)

We don't have the Heart Foundation tick, but our pies would pass. My mate Ralph Plare of Ferguson Plare's Bakery got the tick. But because it costs a few thousand dollars, I didn't bother — but surprisingly enough, lots of pies in Australia would meet that standard.

We use all vegetable margarine in our pastry, and our meat is 100 per cent top-quality steak from the local Beechworth butcher. So our pies are very lean and healthy. Again we use totally scratch recipes, no premixes.

If you get your meat and your pastry right, then you can experiment. You can do Ned Kelly, Pizza Pie, Potato Pie, Mushy Pea Pie with potato, or Curry Pie. It's unlimited, as long as you've got your pastry spot on. You will never need to buy short crust pastry again.

Basic Pie Base

For a basic pie, we want a solid base. For the top of the pie, we use flaky pastry. But the base needs to be made with a denser pastry because it's not just there for decoration.

Preparation time: 15 minutes

Ingredients:

Group 1

Plain flour — $1^3/_4$ cup

Margarine — $^2/_3$ cup

Group 2

Milk — 1 cup

Group 3

Plain flour — 2 cups

Salt — 2 teaspoons

Method:

1. Rub together group 1 very well in large bowl.

2. Add milk, then blend to form a smooth paste.

3. Dry mix group 3 in a separate bowl.

4. Mix all groups together, bring together to form a dough — do not overwork. Roll into a ball.

5. Cover with plastic wrap and allow to rest for 10–15 minutes on bench.

6. Roll out to 1cm thick. Size — to suit your pie dish.

7. Place in greased pie dish.

Plain Steak Pie

With onion, potato, etc.

If you want a meal the kids will love, try a family meat pie with peas, broccoli, potatoes and a few other healthy things. I love a family meat pie with vegetables. What a meal! It tastes wonderful and the kids will eat every bit of it. Dad will love it, Mum will love it — everyone will love it.

Make it yourself and impress the whole family with real Australian fodder. Our best selling pie is the Steak Pie — by far. I would guess that our second best-seller is Steak and Onion, with Steak and Potato coming in third place.

Nevertheless, pies are unlimited. As long as you get a good casing, you can put in whatever filling suits your fancy. If you haven't got mince steak, use minced buffalo — and if you haven't got mince buffalo, try kangaroo.

We use extra lean meat in the Beechworth Bakery pies, so our pie meat has less fat than normal mince meat. Extra lean: we want that E-factor.

We work from a scratch recipe, and we add our own selection of herbs and spices into our pie meats. We do our pies every day, using all fresh ingredients. I've got to live in this town. I've got an incredible reputation for our product and I want to keep it.

Tom's Tip — Puff Pastry

Puff pastry requires a lot of mucking about at home and you would not like me if I gave you the recipe. I suggest you get it conveniently from your local supermarket.

Makes one large family-sized meat pie

Baking time: 20 minutes

Oven temperature: 220°C

Prepare pie base from the preceding Basic Pie Base section, page 65

Ingredients:

Group 1

Minced steak — 400g (prime mince)

Water — 1³/₄ cups

Salt — ¹/₂ teaspoon

Nutmeg — ¹/₄ teaspoon

Caramel colour (chefs call it 'Parisian essence' and we call it 'Blackjack' in the Bakery) — ¹/₄ teaspoon

Pepper — ¹/₄ teaspoon

Tomato Sauce — 1¹/₂ teaspoon

Worcestershire Sauce — 2 teapoons

Group 2

Cornflour — $^1/_4$ cup

Plain flour — 1 tablespoon

Water — $^1/_4$ cup

Method:

1. Place group 1 in a saucepan and bring it to a rolling boil for 5 minutes.

2. Mix together group 2 and stir into group 1 to thicken.

3. Allow mixture to cool before placing it in already prepared pie plate.

4. Top with ready-rolled sheet of puff pastry from your supermarket.

5. Prick top with fork.

6. Bake at 220°C for 20 minutes.

Gourmet Curry Pie

Preparation time: 30 minutes

Baking time: 20-30 minutes

Oven temperature: 220°C

Prepare Basic Pie Base recipe, see earlier in this chapter page 65

Ingredients:

Group 1

Beef chunky/Mince $^1/_2$ each — 300g or $1^1/_4$ cups

Water — $1^1/_4$ cups

Salt — $^1/_4$ teaspoon

Pepper — $^1/_4$ teaspoon

Chicken stock — 1 cube

Curry Powder — $^1/_2$ teaspoon

Potato (diced) — 1 cup

Pumpkin (diced) — 1 cup

Group 2

Half a 430g jar of Sharwood's spicy Tikka Masala or Pataks Original Tikka

Masala — available from your supermarket

Group 3

Water — $1/4$ cup

Cornflour — $1/4$ cup

Plain flour — 1 tablespoon

Caramel Colour — $1/4$ teaspoon (chefs call it 'Parisian essence' and we call it

'Blackjack' in the Bakery)

Method:

1. Place group 1 in saucepan and bring to a rolling boil for 5 minutes.

2. Place group 2 in saucepan and stir with group 1, bring back to boil.

3. Mix group 3 together in a bowl the add to groups 1 and 2 to thicken, stirring all the time.

4. Allow mix to cool before placing in already prepared pie base.

5. Top with a ready-rolled sheet of puff pastry from your supermarket.

6. Prick top of pie with a fork and egg wash.

7. Cook at 220°C for 20 minutes or until golden brown.

Mushroom Pie

Prepare Plain Steak Pie recipe, adding $1/3$ cup of sliced mushrooms lightly fried in 1 tablespoon of butter. Mix in with filling.

Onion Pie

Prepare Plain Steak Pie recipe adding $1/3$ cup lightly fried onions with a pinch of salt and pepper.

Steak & Kidney Pie

Prepare Plain Steak Pie recipe, adding $1/3$ cup of diced kidney. For better flavour, fry the kidney before adding to the meat.

Potato Pie

Anyone can make a Potato Pie; you use your mash potato at home and put it on the top. Or you can use Deb instant potato instead. Topped with cheese and Bacon.

Ned Kelly Pie

I always tell people that I invented the Ned Kelly Pie, but I pinched the recipe off a baker friend called Gary Hudak. Why re-invent the wheel when you can copy? Every baker pinches ideas off the others.

However, Gary didn't call it 'Ned Kelly', he called it 'Egg and Steak'.

But Gary didn't live in Beechworth where Ned and his mum stood trial at the local courthouse. In Beechworth you can buy Ned Kelly cups, cards, key rings and my Ned Kelly Pies. And now they're copied all over the place. Some even call them 'Negg Kelly'; that's pretty rough.

Method:

1. Prepare half Plain Steak Pie recipe filling or make two pies.

2. Place pie filling in prepared pie crust.

3. Crack 3–4 eggs on top of meat filling.

4. Top with $1/_4$ cup grated cheese and $1/_4$ cup of diced bacon. Spread evenly over top of pie.

5. Make sure egg yoke sets when baking (break the yokes before baking if you wish).

Pizza Pie

A Pizza Pie contains meat, capsicum, onion, tomato, cheese and bacon and is absolutely delicious.

Prepare half Plain Steak Pie recipe filling. (Page 65)

Pizza topping:

Diced bacon — $1/_4$ cup

Diced onion — $1/_4$ cup

Chopped red capsicum — $1/_4$ cup

Diced tomato — $1/_4$ cup

Mix together and spread over the top of the pie

Grated cheese — $^1/_3$ cup.

Place cheese over vegetable mix to hold together and stop the vegetable mix from drying out when cooking.

Chicken Pie

Some people prefer a family-sized Chicken Pie to a regular Steak Pie, and sometimes I do too. Chicken is a great alternative to red meat.

Preparation time: 45 minutes

Baking time: 20 minutes

Oven temperature: 220°C

Prepare Basic Pie Base recipe from page 65.

Ingredients:

Group 1

Chicken meat (raw diced) — $^3/_4$ cups

Chicken stock cube — 1

Carrot (grated) — $^1/_4$ cup

Parsley (chopped fine) — 1 teaspoon

Corn — $^1/_4$ cup

Salt — $^1/_2$ teaspoon

Pepper — 1 teaspoon

Water — $1^1/_3$ cups

Group 2

Plain flour — $^1/_4$ cup

Corn flour — 1 tablespoon

Milk — $^1/_2$ cup

Tom's Tip — The Meat In The Middle

Only use good-quality meat in your pies, but you can use too good a quality — you wouldn't put fillet steak in a pie.

Method:

1. Place all of group 1 in a saucepan on the stove and bring to a slow rolling boil for 5–8 minutes to cook the chicken.

2. Dry mix flour and corn flour in group 2. Add milk and mix to form a smooth paste.

3. Add group 2 to group 1 stirring well for 1 minute until thickened.

4. Set aside and allow to cool before placing in pie.

5. Top pie with ready-rolled puff pastry sheet.

6. Press down edge to seal.

7. Puncture holes with fork.

8. Bake at 220°C for 15–18 minutes or until baked.

Caribbean Chicken Pie

Preparation time: 45 minutes

Baking time: 20 minutes

Oven temperature: 220°C

Prepare Basic Pie Base recipe from page 65.

Ingredients:

Group 1

Diced chicken — 300g or $1^1/_4$ cups

Diced carrot — $^1/_3$ cup

Diced onion — $^1/_3$ cup

Diced potato — $^1/_3$ cup

Water — $1^2/_3$ cups

Tomato sauce — 2 teaspoons

Worcestershire Sauce — 2 teaspoons

Chicken stock — 1 cube

Salt — 1 teaspoon

Pepper — 1 teaspoon

Curry powder — 2 teaspoons

Cumin powder — $^1/_2$ teaspoon

Parsley — 1 teaspoon

Group 2

Pineapple crushed — 1 tablespoon

Currants — 1 tablespoon

Diced apple — $^1/_4$ cup

Group 3

Cornflour — $^1/_4$ cup

Water — $^1/_4$ cup

Plain flour — 1 tablespoon

Group 4

Rice — $^1/_4$ cup

Method:

1. Cook rice (group 4) and drain.

2. Place group 1 in saucepan and bring to a rolling boil for five minutes.

3. Add group 2, return to a rolling boil for two minutes.

4. Mix group 3 to a smooth paste in a bowl, then stir group 3 into groups 1 and 2 as it is boiling to thicken chicken mix. Then mix in cooked rice.

5. Allow mix to cool a bit before placing in already prepared pie base.

6. Top pie with ready-rolled sheet of puff pastry from your supermarket.

7. Press down edge to seal and prick top with fork.

8. Cook at 220°C for 20 minutes or until golden brown.

Steak & Black Pepper Pie

There's more to a Steak & Black Pepper Pie than just chucking in a whole lot of black pepper into a steak pie. That's why I've given you a separate recipe.

Makes one family-sized pie

Baking time: 20 minutes

Oven temperature: 220°C

Prepare Basic Pie Base from recipe page 65.

Ingredients:

Group 1

Diced steak — 200g

Minced steak — 200g (prime mince)

Water — $1^1/_2$ cups

Salt — $^1/_2$ teaspoon

Nutmeg — $^1/_4$ teaspoon

Caramel colour ('Parisian essence' or 'Blackjack') — $^1/_4$ teaspoon

Group 2

Cornflour — $^1/_4$ cup

Plain flour — 1 tablespoon

Water — $^1/_4$ cup

Group 3

Cream — $^1/_4$ cup

Cracked pepper — 1 teaspoon

Method:

1. Place group 1 in a saucepan on the stove. Bring to a rolling boil and allow to boil for 5–8 minutes.

2. Combine group 2 then stir into group 1 to thicken.

3. Combine group 3 into meat mix.

4. Allow meat mixture to cool. Then place in prepared pie plate.

5. Place filling in lined pie plate. Top with ready rolled puff pastry sheets.

6. Prick top with a fork.

7. Bake at 220°C for 20 minutes.

Roast Vegie Quiche

This one's a great one, invented by Dianne Forrest. Use what you like, if you hate onion don't have it, however, if you love roast parsnip go for it. This is what we have with ours.

Preparation time: 25 minutes

Baking time (roasting vegies): 18-20 minutes

Baking time (quiche): 50-60 minutes

Oven temperature: 200°C

Prepare Base Pie Base pastry from page 65.

Group 1 — Roast vegies

1 medium potato

$^1/_2$ carrot

$^1/_2$ parsnip

$^1/_2$ small swede

small piece of pumpkin

oil — 2 tablespoons

Minced garlic — 1 teaspoon

Black pepper — $^1/_2$ teaspoon

Group 2

Grated tasty cheese — $^1/_2$ cup

Diced onion — $^1/_3$ cup

Broccoli bits — 4 to 5 or $^1/_2$ cup

Curry powder — $^1/_2$ teaspoon

Group 3 — Liquid filling

Eggs — 2

Cream — $^1/_3$ cup

Milk — $^1/_3$ cup

Salt — $^1/_2$ teaspoon

Method:

1. Pre-heat oven to 220°C.

2. Slice all vegies in group 1, mix all group 1 together and spread over tray and roast in oven for 18-20 minutes.

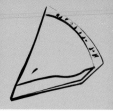
3.   Allow to partly cool and mix all of group 2 together with vegies in a bowl.

4.   Place all this mix in prepared base in quiche or pie dish.

5.   Whisk group 3 together in a bowl and add to filling.

6.   Gently place in oven at 200°C for 50-60 minutes or until baked.

Tom's Tip

Place a tray on next rack down, under quiche in oven to avoid making a mess from spillage.

Vegetable Medley Pie

Our Vegetable Medley Pie is superb. It's the only way you can describe it, whether you like vegetarian food or not.

Prepare Basic Pie Base recipe see page 65.

Preparation time: $1/_2$ hour

Oven temperature: 200°C

Baking time: 30–40 minutes

Ingredients:

Group 1

Diced zucchini — $1/_2$ cup

Diced carrot — $1/_2$ cup

Diced pumpkin — $1/_2$ cup

Broccoli — 1 cup loose

Diced potato — $1/_2$ cup

Group 2

Mashed potato — $2/_3$ cup, dry mashed, no milk or butter added

Salt and pepper or garlic/mixed herbs — to taste

Butter melted — 1 tablespoon

Diced onion — $1/_2$ cup

Peas — $^1/_2$ cup

Corn — $^1/_2$ cup

Cream — $^1/_4$ cup

Egg — 1 @ 55g

Grated cheese tasty — $^2/_3$ cup + $^1/_4$ cup for topping

Method:

1. Place large pot of water on stove, bring to boil.

2. Dice up vegies of group 1; blanch in hot water for 5 minutes.

3. Drain vegies well and mix with all other ingredients.

4. Place mix in prepared pie dish.

5. Top with grated cheese.

6. Bake in oven 200°C for 30–40 minutes, or until cooked.

Spinach Fetta Rolls

Spinach Fetta Rolls weren't around in the old days. They started becoming popular when people started to travel overseas, and when they came back to Australia they asked, "Where can we get spinach and fetta rolls from?" And after a while the bakeries responded, "Right here".

Preparation time: $^1/_2$ hour

Oven temperature: 240°C

Baking time: 15–18 minutes

Ingredients:

Frozen spinach or fresh fine chopped — 1 cup

Egg — 1 @ 55g

Breadcrumbs — $^2/_3$ cup

Cheese tasty grated — 1 cup

Fetta cheese — 1 cup crumbed

Onion fresh — $^1/_4$ cup grated

Salt — $^1/_4$ teaspoon

Pepper — $1/_4$ teaspoon

Pasta cooked — $3/_4$ cup small shells

Potato mash — $1^1/_2$ cups, dry no milk or butter added

Method:

1. Cook pasta, then add all ingredients and mix well. This could make pasties, or a pie or two. Roll up like sausage rolls (see later in this chapter).

Suggestion: Use this filling to make pies, pasties, vegetarian lasagne or a pasta sauce

Quiche Lorraine

Who says, "Real men don't eat quiche". We sell heaps of them, to all sorts of blokes.

Variation

For Vegetarian Quiche, substitute bacon with $3/_4$ cup of mushroom or $1/_3$ cup asparagus, well drained.

To make one large quiche

Preparation time: 25 minutes

Baking time: 50–60 minutes

Oven temperature: 200°C

Ingredients for filling:

Prepare the Basic Pie Base recipe Page 65 and roll out to 1cm thick and line pie dish or flan tin

Group 1

Bacon — $1/_2$ cup

Cheese — $3/_4$ cup

Diced onion — $1/_2$ cup

Fresh diced tomato — $1/_2$ cup

Parsley — 2 teaspoons

Group 2

Eggs @ 50g — 2

Milk — $1/_3$ cup

Cream — $1/_3$ cup

Salt — $1/_2$ teaspoon

Pepper — $1/_2$ teaspoon

Method:

1. Mix together group 1 and place in pie dish.

2. Whisk together group 2 and pour over group 1 in pie dish.

3. Bake in oven at 200°C for 50–60 minutes or until cooked.

Meat Pastie

The Pastie originated in Cornwall where the real old-fashioned recipe recommends using turnip, swede and parsnip as ingredients. The Pastie has been changed in its travels around the world. You can make Tuna Pastie, Salmon Pastie and any pastie you want. You can make big pasties, little pasties or pasties of any size.

As long as your pastry is good, you can add any filling. If you want meat pasties, get quality mince meat and don't use too much. And always use the freshest vegetables.

Makes: 8 small pasties

Preparation time: 20 minutes

Baking time: 15–20 minutes

Oven temperature: 210°C

Ingredients:

Salt — $1/_4$ teaspoon

Pepper — $1/_4$ teaspoon

Breadcrumbs — $3/_4$ cup

Garlic powder (or one clove) — $1/_4$ teaspoon

Prime mince beef — $3/_4$ cup (200 g)

Onion (finely chopped) — 1 cup

Carrot (finely diced or grated) — 1 cup

Potato (finally diced or grated) — $1^1/_2$ cup

Eggs — 2

Frozen peas — $1/_2$ cup

Puff pastry sheets — 4 readymade sheets

Method:

1. Pre-heat oven to 210°C.

2. Using premade pastry sheets from supermarket, cut in half.

3. Mix together all ingredients.

4. Using an ice cream scoop or tablespoon, scoop out mixture, and place to one side on pastry. Lightly brush sides with water and fold and join together.

5. Place on greased oven tray.

6. Prick top with fork and glaze with milk on top.

7. Bake at 210°C for approximately 15–20 minutes.

8. Serve while warm.

Variations

1. To make family-sized pastie, use full sheet of puff pastry.

2. Place filling in centre and flatten to approximately 2cm thick.

3. Fold pastry seams together, turn over and place on greased oven tray. Prick with fork. Glaze with milk.

4. Bake at 210°C for approximately 15-20 minutes.

Tom's Tip

Try eggwash to give a nice glaze over pastry. Don't apply too heavily as it will burn.

Eggwash Recipe

Ingredients:

1 egg

Milk —1$\frac{1}{4}$ cup

Salt — $\frac{1}{4}$ teaspoon

Method:

Beat together and paint lightly on pastry before baking.

Bushman Pasties

Makes 3 large pasties

Preparation time: 20 minutes

Baking time: 30-35 minutes

Oven temperature: 210°C

This is a Bushman Pastie — it is a big feed. One will do a meal on its own, kids may eat half of one.

Tom's Tip

Use a food processor to cut the vegetables up, cuts the time down and vegetables are more of an even size, we do $1/_2$ cubed and $1/_2$ grated.

Ingredients:

Group 1

Breadcrumbs — $3/_4$ cup

Garlic — $1/_2$ teaspoon

Salt —1 teaspoon

Pepper — 1 teaspoon

Peas (frozen) — $1/_2$ cup

Corn (frozen) — $1/_2$ cup

Group 2

Potatoes (diced) — 2 cups

Carrots (diced) — $3/_4$ cup

Onion (diced) — 1 cup

Spinach (chopped) — $1/_3$ cup

Group 3

Parsnip (grated) — $3/_4$ cup

Swede (grated) — $3/_4$ cup

Puff Pastry (from supermarket) — 3 sheets

Method:

1. Place group 1 in a bowl, dice group 2, grate group 3.

2. Add all groups together, mix with your hands, it may seem dry at first but this will paste up and come together so when a handful is squeezed, it stays together like wet sand.

3. Lay out pastry on lightly flowered bench, place 1 cup of the mix across pastry sheet left to right and form a shape like an up turned row boat.

4. Take up top and bottom of sheet and pinch together to make a fin.

5. From end to end use your fingers to zig zag the fin to make it look like a croc's back, pinch the ends closed. (Like photo on page 63).

6. Egg wash pastry.

7. Place on baking tray and let rest for 10 minutes before baking.

8. Cook at 210°C for 30–35 minutes or until golden brown.

Sausage Rolls

Sausage Rolls are not pure meat. The filling is a combination of sausage mince, breadcrumbs and seasoning. The breadcrumbs stops the shrinking of the meat and keeps in the moisture.

Preparation time: 20 minutes,

Baking time: 15–20 minutes,

Oven temperature: 220°C

Filling:

Salt and pepper — 1 teaspoon of each

Chicken stock cube — 1

Onion grated (small) — $^1/_4$ cup

Sausage mince — 1 cup

Prime mince — 1 cup

Breadcrumbs — 2 cups

Water (warm) — 2 cups

Carrot (grates) — $^2/_3$ cups

Worcestershire Sauce — 1 tablespoon

Pastry — $3^1/_2$ puff pastry sheets, (24cm x 24cm) cut in half.

Method:

1. Pre-heat oven to 220°C.

2. Dissolve stock cube in water.

3. Combine all ingredients except pastry and mix well.

4. Using puff pastry sheets, cut in half, 12cm x 24cm strips.

5. Pipe out line (diameter of a 20 cent piece) of mixture onto puff pastry sheet and roll up, cut in half, making 14 Sausage Rolls.

6. Place on tray, seam down, brush top with water and add sesame seeds (optional).

7. Bake at 220°CC for 15–20 minutes.

Variation

For something different, add mixed herbs, chilli sauce or powder, topped with sesame seeds.

Utility Cake, Walnut and Sultana Loaf, Carrot Cake, Banana Cake, Chocolate Moist Beetroot Cake, Canadian Date Cake (or Slice), Christmas Festive Fruit Cake, Murray Mud Cake, Dutch Apple Cake.

caked in success

If you don't feel good about yourself, I don't think you can make a good cake. You've got to have that passion if you want to turn out something nice for your family and your friends. It can't be a chore. It's not a 'job' like the washing or the ironing, which is totally ungratifying. If you do a beautiful cake, everyone will love you.

You've got to have that belief in yourself that "I can make the apple sponge. I can do this apricot crumble. I can do it; it's not rocket science. I can do it." Often we think, "It's too hard", because a lot of recipes make it sound like it's too hard. It's not hard, it's just a matter of getting in there and doing it.

A fresh cake is there to eat, it's not there to keep. And the freshness makes all the difference, that's for sure.

A lot of bakers keep their product too long. They keep it two days after they should have chucked it. Many cooks make a beautiful fresh product, then they leave it out the back until tomorrow. The same applies at home.

I think kids are the best judges of cakes. If kids love your cakes, those cakes are spot on.

However, you mustn't make them too sweet. Most Australians do not go for American cakes, when it comes to cakes we have European and English tastes. Most of our Aussie recipes originated from our early settlers who were from mostly English and Irish descent. We are probably still following and developing along the same lines today, adapting to our conditions and multicultural influences.

I love oven-finished cakes, like Dutch Apple Cake and Sultana Loaf. You pull them out of the oven and yum.

Then you've got Ginger Cake.

You've got Chocolate Cake.

You've got Murray Mud Cake.

You've got Chocolate Pecan Cake.

You've got Coffee Cake.

Our cakes are not like French patisserie; they are classical Australian home baking. Anyone can follow our recipe and they'll make a really good product. French patisserie might need 20 steps, whereas we try and keep it simple.

In 2000, the Beechworth Bakery baked three large sponge and cream cakes, to raise money for the Paralympics, when the Olympic Torch ran through Albury. There were lots of people around, and Dianne Forrest decorated those cakes to make them spectacular. Her heart was in it, and the sky was her limit!

The first pattern depicted a country scene of hills, cars, horses and the Beechworth Bakery; the second and third were sporting images featuring an athlete, the Olympic logo and the words 'Albury–Wodonga, Gateway To The Games'. These were photo cakes, with the photo-image transferred onto edible rice paper using food colouring.

The crowd was really impressed by those cakes. Cakes are naturally impressive anyway.

Utility Cake

Out of our 'Utility Mix' you can make Cupcakes, Bar Cake, Butterfly Cake and you can also make your Lamingtons. You can also do Apple Sponges and Apple Crumble Sponges. Well...we might call it a 'sponge', but it's not really — in this instance, it's a utility mix — it's very useful and versatile.

Preparation time: 10 minutes

Oven temperature: 160°C

Baking time: 40–45 minutes

Ingredients:

Butter — $1^1/_4$ cups

Castor sugar — $1^1/_2$ cups

Salt — $1^1/_2$ teaspoons

Eggs @ 50g — 6

Baking powder — 3 teaspoons

Warm milk — $^1/_2$ cup

Vanilla — 1 tablespoon

Plain flour — $3^1/_3$ cups

Vegetable oil — $2^1/_2$ tablespoons

Method:

1. Preheat oven to 160°C.

2. Beat butter in castor sugar until light and fluffy.

3. Mix in a separate dish eggs and oil, then add to butter/sugar mixture, a little at a time, and beat in.

4. In a separate dish, sift together salt, baking powder and cake flour. Add this slowly to the other mixture, blending as you do this for approximately 30 seconds.

5. Add milk, vanilla essence and blend together for approximately 3 minutes until smooth.

6. Place in greased cup, cake tins or greased glass pie plate (large). This mix will make two 20cm cakes with fruit on top, e.g. apricot, apple, rhubarb or whatever you prefer.

7. Add fruit of your choice on top, then sprinkle cinnamon and sugar mixture on top.

8. Bake at 160°C for 40–45 minutes. Turn in oven when half-cooked.

Topping:

Fruit of choice, $^3/_4$ cup

Cinnamon, 1 teaspoon

Castor sugar, 3 tablespoons

Walnut and Sultana Loaf

Everyone does their own thing with Walnut and Sultana Loaf. Some people cover it in thick butter and Golden Syrup for their midnight munchies.

Preparation time: 20 minutes

Baking time: 1 hour and 10 minutes

Oven temperature: 150°C

Ingredients:

Sultanas — 1 cup

Brown sugar — $^3/_4$ cup

Margarine — $^1/_4$ cup

Golden Syrup — 1 tablespoon

Egg — 1

Plain flour — 2 cups

Baking powder — 2 teaspoons

Mixed spice — 1 teaspoon

Ginger — 1 teaspoon

Nutmeg — 1 teaspoon

Walnuts — 80g or $^1/_2$ cup

Milk (warm) — $^3/_4$ cup

Method:

1. Pre-heat oven to 150°C.

2. Soak sultanas in warm milk for 10 minutes.

3. Cream together sugar, margarine, Golden Syrup.

4. Add egg, beat until mixed in, until light and smooth.

5. Add soaked sultanas and milk mixture.

6. Sieve dry ingredients, then add to mixture and beat in.

7. Add chopped walnuts, mix through.

8. Pour into loaf tin.

9. Bake in oven at 150°C for 1 hour and 10 minutes. May require covering with foil if it is becoming too dark on top.

Carrot Cake

Carrot Cake is an American classic. When you think about that, it is unusual, because it is made from a root vegetable, which is seldom used in desserts. But the carrot makes it moist, and at the bakery we also add pineapple juice.

For a non-cream cake, I love our Carrot Cake. I think it's something special. It is best if it has also got Carrot Cake Icing. That beautiful icing makes it fair dinkum.

Baking time: 1 hour and 45 minutes

Oven temperature: 160°C

Preparation time: 25 minutes

Ingredients:

Apple, diced — 1 cup

Carrots, grated — $2^1/_4$ cups (soft packed)

Walnuts, broken — $^3/_4$ cup

Sultanas — $3/4$ cup

Brown sugar — 2 cups (soft packed)

Eggs — 3 x 50g

Vegetable oil — $2/3$ cup

Vanilla essence — 1 teaspoon

Plain flour — $2^1/_2$ cups

Cinnamon — 1 teaspoon

Mixed spices — 3 teaspoons

Bicarb soda — 2 teaspoons

Cold water — 2 teaspoons

Method:

1.   Pre-heat oven at 160°C.

2.   Prepare cake tin — grease tin and line bottom with greaseproof paper.

3.   Mix together apple, carrots, walnuts, sultanas, brown sugar.

4.   Then add eggs, vegetable oil and vanilla essence and mix together well.

5.   Dissolve bicarb soda in water. Add this to mixture along with flour cinnamon and mixed spice. Mix together thoroughly then place in tin and bake at 160°C for approximately 1 hour and 40 minutes.

Carrot Cake Icing

Ingredients:

Icing sugar — 2 cups

Vanilla essence — 2 teaspoons

Margarine — $1/3$ cup

Cream cheese — $1/3$ cup

Crushed walnuts (for topping) — $1/2$ cup

Method:

1. Beat margarine, cream cheese, icing sugar and vanilla together until light and fluffy.

2. Spread over top of cake when cake has cooled.

3. Sprinkle with crushed walnuts.

Banana Cake

One of the secrets of Banana Cake is using over-ripe banana. When you get them over-ripe at home, instead of chucking them, put them in the freezer. Although they'll be mushy and they'll go black, the insides will be great for Banana Cake.

Preparation time: 20 minutes

Baking time: 30–35 minutes

Oven temperature: 180°C

Ingredients:

Group 1

Ripe bananas (mashed) — $^3/_4$ cup or 2 bananas

Brown sugar or castor sugar — $^3/_4$ cup

Group 2

Egg — 1 @ 55g

Vanilla essence — $^1/_2$ teaspoon

Group 3

Plain flour — $^3/_4$ cup

Salt — $^1/_4$ teaspoon

Cinnamon — $^1/_2$ teaspoon

Bicarb soda — 1 teaspoon

Group 4

Milk — $1^1/_2$ tablespoons

Vegetable oil — $1^1/_2$ tablespoons

Method:

1. Pre-heat oven — 180°C.

2. Mix group 1 together.

3. Add group 2 and mix well.

4. Sift group 3 together.

5. Blend group 3 with groups 1 and 2.

Tom's Tip — Always Wash Your Dried Fruit (sultanas, currants, raisins, etc.)

Wash your fruit (first in warm water, then in cold) before using it as ingredients. People say, "Why wash Australian fruit?" Australian fruit is very clean; it's all pre-washed — it even says 'washed fruit' on the box. Nevertheless, at the bakery, we wash it because this softens the fruit. (Dry fruit takes a lot of moisture out of the cake batter.) Then we put the fruit into a sieve and let ot sit for a a few hours until all the water has drained — the fruit will absorb some of that moisture.

6. Add in group 4. Mix until smooth.

7. Pour into grease loaf tin — 21cm by 11cm.

8. Bake at 180°C for 30–35 minutes.

9. When baked, turn out and allow to cool on cake wire.

10. Dust with icing sugar when cooled.

Chocolate Moist Beetroot Cake

The inclusion of beetroot in a cake might sound odd, but it's there to keep the cake moist. Nobody likes dry cake.

Preparation time: 25 minutes

Baking time: 40–50 minutes

Oven temperature: 150°C

Ingredients:

Eggs — 2 @ 66g

Vegetable oil — $^1/_2$ cup

Plain flour — 1 cup

Cocoa — 2 tablespoons

Bicarb soda — $^3/_4$ teaspoon

Castor sugar — $^3/_4$ cup

Salt — $^3/_4$ teaspoon

Vanilla essence — $^1/_2$ teaspoon

Tinned beetroot (shredded and drained) — $^3/_4$ cup or 425g tin

Baking Powder — 2 teaspoons

Method:

1. Pre-heat oven at 150°C.

2. Beat egg and oil together.

3. In a separate bowl sift flour, cocoa, bicarb soda, baking powder, castor sugar and salt.

4. Combine egg mixture to sifted ingredients. Add vanilla essence and mix in.

5. Add tinned shredded beetroot and mix well.

6. Place in greased cake tin.

7. Bake at 150°C for 40–50 minutes.

8. Allow to cool.

9. Add topping.

Topping:

Cocoa powder — 2 tablespoons

Icing sugar — $1^1/_2$ cups

Softened butter — $^1/_2$ cup

Milk — 1 tablespoon

Beat until light and fluffy, spread over cake.

Canadian Date Cake (or Slice)

I don't know why it's called Canadian Date Cake. It's too cold to grow dates in Canada.

Makes: 1

Baking time: 30 minutes

Oven temperature: 150°C

Ingredients:

Dates (pitted and chopped) — 1 cup

Hot water (boiling) — $^1/_2$ cup

Bicarb soda — 2 teaspoons

Sugar (castor) — $^3/_4$ cup

Butter (softened) — $^1/_3$ cup

Egg — 1

Plain flour — $1^1/_3$ cup

Salt — $^1/_4$ teaspoon

Tinned apple — 1 tin (420g)

Tom's Tip — Fresh, Fresh, Fresh

The fresher your baking soda, the better your cake.

Method:

1. Pre-heat oven to 150°C.

2. Dissolve bicarb soda in water and add dates to soak for 15 minutes.

3. Cream butter and castor sugar together.

4. Add eggs and beat through until light and fluffy.

5. Sift salt and flour, and combine with creamed butter/sugar mixture. Add tinned apple and date mixture and mix thoroughly.

6. Pour into greased and lined cake tin.

7. Prepare topping.

8. Bake cake partially until firm to touch (approximately 30–35 minutes) then remove from oven and spread topping over top, then return to oven for a further 10 minutes at 150°C to cook topping.

9. Allow to cool in tin for approximately 20 minutes then turn out on cooling wire and allow to cool.

Topping:

Brown sugar (not raw) — 1 cup (softly packed)

Butter — $^1/_3$ cup

Coconut shredded — $1^3/_4$ cup

Milk — $^1/_4$ cup

Method:

1. Place milk, butter and brown sugar in saucepan, stir together and bring to a rolling boil.

2. Take off stove, add coconut and mix well.

3. Spread over cake.

Christmas festive fruit Cake

We do 4000 cakes every Christmas and they're all hand done. People say, "Tom, it's not worth making Christmas Cakes; anyone can go out and buy a cheap Christmas Cake, Lions has got it all." But when you buy a cake from a bakery there's a lot more love and care gone into it than a factory cake.

And all around Australia, every small bakery's Christmas Cakes are probably hand done, just like ours.

I love doing my Christmas cakes. I love getting my hands in the batter. And I love knowing that every one of those cakes will give a lot of joy to families, and that's pretty special to me.

Our festive fruit cake is a very old recipe that's been around for a long time.

One of the secrets with Christmas Cakes is the washing of the fruit, the glistenating and putting the fruit in the rum two days before we glistenate. Then we put our festive fruit topping on the top, (glazed red and green cherries, glazed pineapple, mixed peel and flaked almond).

It's a real festive look, and it's been a real winner for us. So come in and get one. We also mail order them, or order one on the internet around October–December:

www.beechworthbakery.com

Pre-preparation time: 2 days

Baking time: 4 hours 15 minutes

Preparation time: 40 minutes

Oven temperature: 140°C

Ingredients:

Butter — 1 cup

Brown sugar — 1 cup

Tom's Tip — Real Rum

When a recipe says 'add rum', use real rum not rum essence. Although the alcohol all goes out with the cooking, the taste is more authentic.

Eggs — 5 x 60g or 6 x 50g

Cornflour — 1 tablespoon

Plain flour — 2$\frac{1}{4}$ cups

Nutmeg — 1 teaspoon

Mixed spice — 1 teaspoon

Sultanas — 2 cups

Raisins — 1$\frac{2}{3}$ cups

Currants — 1 cup

Pecan nuts (broken) — $\frac{2}{3}$ cup

Mixed peel — $\frac{1}{2}$ cup (optional)

Glazed cherries (red) — $\frac{1}{3}$ cup

Glazed cherries (green) — $\frac{1}{3}$ cup

Parisian essence — 3 teaspoons

Rum — $\frac{1}{4}$ cup

Glycerine — 1 tablespoon

Baking powder — 1$\frac{1}{2}$ teaspoon

Preparation Method:

1. Wash and drain dry fruit together (sultanas, raisins and currants).

2. Dry well on a tea towel.

3. Cut cherries into halves.

4. Mix together in a large bowl: washed fruit, cherries, mixed peel, pecans, rum and glycerine.

5. Cover and allow to stand for 2 days, giving a mix each day.

6. After fruit is ready, prepare tin (20cm square or 22.5cm round tin).

7. Grease tin and line with 2 pieces of grease proof paper. Line outside of tin with thick cardboard, e.g. cut cardboard to shape of outside of tin, including base and sides, and tie with wire or string.

At the bakery, we cook Christmas Cakes in special made wooden boxes, so the cake does not dry out around the edges. So it is important to line the cake tin with cardboard.

8. Place plain flour, cornflour, nutmeg, mixed spice and baking powder in a bowl and sift together twice.

9. Now down to it with all the prep work done.

Ingredients for topping:

Flaked almonds — $1/_3$ cup

Mixed peel — $1/_4$ cup (optional)

Glazed pineapple — $1/_4$ cup

Glazed red cherries — $1/_3$ cup

Glazed green cherries — $1/_3$ cup

Chop up cherries into $1/_2$ size, also chop pineapple to this size. Mix all ingredients together.

Method:

1. Preheat oven 140°C.

2. Cream butter with brown sugar until light and fluffy.

3. Beat in one egg at a time, adding a tablespoon of dry ingredient with each egg.

4. When all eggs are added, beat in Parisian essence.

5. Add in the remainder of the dry ingredient slowly, mixing in until clear (clear — bakery talk for all mixed in together. No more wet or dry ingredients to be seen, but mixed together).

6. Fold fruit in by hand until clear.

7. Place in prepared cake tin.

8. With a damp hand, press mix evenly into tin.

9. Place topping mix on top of cake, pressing in a little.

10. Bake in oven at 140°C for 4 hours and 15 minutes.

11. Turn cake in oven once every hour making sure topping is not getting too dark.

12. If the topping is getting too dark, cover with tin foil.

13. Check cake is cooked with skewer as oven time may vary from oven to oven, e.g. electric, gas, fan forced (we used an electric fan forced oven).

14. When cake comes out of oven, melt some apricot jam in small saucepan and glaze the top of the cake.

Murray Mud Cake

I have a property on the Murray River and there's lots of mud there. It squeezes between my toes and reminds me of my childhood.

I looked at a recipe for a Mississippi Mud cake and thought, "We're on the Murray. I'm not going to call my cakes after another country's river!"

Our Murray Mud Cake is very rich. It's right up there with our best-sellers, but it's not one of my favourites. It frustrates me. You can only eat a small bit, but I want to eat a big bit — that's why I take it easy with this one.

Preparation time: 30 minutes

Baking time: 45–40 minutes

Oven temperature: 160°C

Ingredients:

Group 1

Castor sugar — $1\frac{1}{4}$ cups

Margarine — $\frac{1}{2}$ cup

Group 2

Eggs — 3

Vegetable oil — $\frac{1}{2}$ cup

Milk — $\frac{1}{2}$ cup

Imitation chocolate essence — 1 tablespoon

Group 3

Plain flour — $1\frac{1}{3}$ cups

Cocoa powder — $\frac{2}{3}$ cup

Baking powder — 1 teaspoon

Bicarb soda — $\frac{1}{4}$ teaspoon

Salt — 1 teaspoon

Method:

1. Pre-heat oven to 160°C.

2. Sift together group 3.

3. While creaming together group 1, slowly add in group 2.

4. When groups 1 and 2 are mixed together, blend in group 3.

5. Pour into greased tin and bake at 160°C for 45–50 minutes or until baked. This cake should be moist.

6. Allow to cool for 10 minutes in tin before turning out onto cake wire.

Gnache Ingredients (Rich Chocolate Sauce)

Cream — 1 cup

Butter — 1 tablespoon

Chocolate buds — 300g

Method for gnache:

1. Place cream and butter in saucepan on medium heat.

2. Bring to rolling boil, melting butter.

3. Add chocolate buds mixing well until buds are melted.

4. Remove from heat and pour chocolate sauce into jug and allow to cool on bench for 15–20 minutes.

5. When cake is cooled, cut in half (horizontally) and fill with one third of the garnish.

6. Place cake onto a tray and pour the remaining two thirds of the chocolate sauce over the cake — cover the whole cake.

Tip: Chocolate sauce may have to be reheated in microwave if it is too set to pour.

Variation

Instead of using chocolate essence, use rum essence and make a rum cake instead, and make a rum sauce.

PS. Or try brandy.

Dutch Apple Cake

They don't call it Dutch Apple Cake because the apples are Dutch, but because the Dutch East India Company supplied cinnamon during the 17th century, when it had 150 trading ships at sea.

Preparation time: 20 minutes

Baking time: 1 hour and 20 minutes

Oven temperature: 150°C

Ingredients:

Castor sugar — $^1/_3$ cup

Brown sugar — $^1/_3$ cup

Margarine — $^1/_3$ cup

Golden Syrup — 2 tablespoons

Egg — 1 (60g)

Plain flour — 2 cups

Baking powder — 2 teaspoons

Mixed spice — 2 teaspoons

Ginger — $1^1/_2$ teaspoons

Nutmeg — $1^1/_2$ teaspoons

Tinned apple — 1 cup or 250g

Cinnamon — 3 teaspoons

Milk — 1 cup

Extra apple (for topping) — $^1/_3$ cup

Method:

1.   Pre-heat oven to 150°C.

2.   Cream together castor sugar, Golden Syrup and margarine.

3.   Add egg and beat until smooth.

4.   Add 1 cup of apple.

5.   In a separate bowl, sieve dry ingredients, then combine with creamed mixture adding milk and mix together.

6.   Pour into greased cake tin. Add extra apple over top.

7.   Add crumble topping and pat down gently.

8.   Bake at 150°C for 1 hour and 20 minutes.

Topping Crumble:

Rub together the following ingredients:

Coconut — $\frac{1}{2}$ cup

Margarine — 1 tablespoon

Castor sugar — 1 tablespoon

Cinnamon — $\frac{1}{2}$ teaspoon

Caramel Slice, Hedgehog Slice, Lemon Slice, Vanilla Slice, French Vanilla Slice, Peppermint Slice, Tuscany Slice

slices of life

A slice is like a big, fat, giant biscuit — (one slice equals four to six biscuits). You can eat half now and half later. Or share it with someone you like, after which they're sure to like you!

What slices have in common is not the flour, but the principle of 'layering' the ingredients — layers of either shortbread, fillings or icings. They all have a top and a bottom. Some have cooked tops or cooked bottoms, some are not cooked at all, and others have cooked tops and bottoms with fillings in between. So there are all types.

So there is a wide range of flour in this section. A lot of them have got shortbread bases.

Caramel Slice

Caramel Slices are not hard to do, but they're a bloody hassle if you make stupid mistakes.

So don't burn them — caramel sugar always smells terrible when it's burnt. You'll never get rid of the smell before Aunt Dolly calls round.

And don't drop it on your kitchen floor. It's a sticky mess to clean up, like honey. That's my first tip — although not quite the power of positive thinking.

Baking time — 12–15 minutes

Oven temperature: 180°C

Ingredients:

Condensed milk — 4 cups

Golden Syrup — 1 cup

Margarine melted — $1/_3$ cup

Chocolate (for topping) — 1 cup or 250g

Method:

Pre-heat oven to 180°C.

Base:

1. Prepare half mix of shortbread from biscuit recipe, following steps 1–4 then roll out to 1cm thick.

2. Line base of slice tray (approximate tray size: 25cm by 34cm, $2^1/_2$cm deep).

3. Pre-bake base, lightly.

Filling:

1. Melt margarine and Golden Syrup together in saucepan.

2. Add to condensed milk, mix together.

3. Spread evenly over lightly pre-baked shortbread base.

4. Bake until caramel sets 12–15 mins at 180ºC.

5. Allow to cool. Spread melted chocolate over top.

6. Cut into squares or fingers before chocolate sets to hard.

Hedgehog Slice

Hedgehogs are made with old broken biscuits — Marie Biscuits are best, but anything will do. The 'hedgehog' idea is a kiddies thing, but adults love them too.

I can't Australianise this one because everyone understands that it's called Hedgehog Slice because that's what it looks like. But if I called it Echidna Slice, everyone would think it was a savoury product.

Preparation time: 20 minutes

Ingredients:

Group 1

Egg — 3 x 55g

Castor sugar — $1\frac{1}{2}$ cups

Group 2

Desiccated coconut — 2 cups

Cocoa powder — $\frac{2}{3}$ cup

Group 3

Copha — $1\frac{1}{4}$ cups, just melted, not too hot

Group 4

Biscuits — 450g/or 40–45 biscuits

You can use broken ones

Method:

1. Beat group 1 till smooth.

2. Add group 2 and blend together.

3. Do not over heat group 3 as this will cook the egg mixture.

4. Add in copha and mix in very well.

5. Add in broken biscuits. Blend together with your hand or wooden spoon — as you do not wish to have the biscuits broken up too much or the slice to go dry.

6. Press out into slice tray quickly before the mixture cools and sets.

Topping:

Cocoa powder — $1/_4$ cup

Icing sugar — 2 cups

Soft butter — $2/_3$ cup

Mix together and top slice — cut into fingers or squares.

Lemon Slice

A lot of people like to have a lemon drink in winter for their Vitamin C. Matthew McLaurin eats Lemon Slices instead.

Ingredients:

Condensed milk — 1 tin (395/400g)

Marie Biscuits — 3 packs or 750g

Desiccated coconut — $2^1/_3$ cups

Rind of two lemons grated

Juice of one lemon

Butter — tub 375g

Method:

1. Melt butter, combine all ingredients adding biscuits last. Take care not to break biscuits up too small much as they will dry the slice out.

2. Press into slice tray and allow to cool and set in freezer.

3. Remove from freezer, turn out and ice — using icing recipe below.

Icing:

$1/_4$ cup of lemon juice (warm in microwave)

$1/_4$ cup soft butter (warm in microwave)

3 cups of icing sugar (sifted)

Mix together till light and smooth and top slice. Then cut into fingers or squares.

Vanilla Slice

You can do many things with pastry sheets, and Vanilla Slice is one of them. There's a bit of an art to pastry sheets. You've got to 'dock' them well — which is when you put in the holes with a fork. If you don't put in the holes the pastry will become flaky.

Once you've got it right you can do Napoleons, French Vanilla and Vanilla Slice.

You can do a lot of things, like Vanilla Slice as a Birthday Cake. That's Marty Matassoni's idea actually. It was an idea he got after a cousin recently ordered a Vanilla Slice Wedding Cake.

Baking time: 13–15 minutes

Oven temperature: 220°C

Ingredients:

Group 1

Milk — $1^2/_3$ cup

Cream — $1^2/_3$ cup

Castor sugar — 1 cup

Butter — $^2/_3$ cup

Group 2

Cornflour — $1^1/_4$ cups

Milk — $^2/_3$ cup

Vanilla essence — 3 teaspoon

Yellow colouring — 2 drops

Puff pastry, ready rolled sheets — 2 (buy it from your supermarket)

Method:

1. Place puff pastry sheets on greased oven tray. Place fork holes all over pastry.

2. Bake in oven at 220°C for 13–15 minutes.

3. Combine group 1 and place in saucepan and bring to rolling boil. Do not boil over. Ensure the butter has melted.

4. Combine all of group 2 in a bowl and mix until lump free. Then pour group 2 into group 1 while still on stove and stir well until it has thickened.

5. Pour custard onto one of the pastry sheets in a deep slice tray.

6. Level out custard, then place other sheet of pastry on top (smooth side up).

7. Place a tray on top (with a weight on it) and allow to set in refrigerator for half an hour.

8. Ice with desired topping or alternatively dust with icing sugar.

9. Cut up to desired size.

Vanilla Slice Topping:

Icing sugar — 1 cup

Soft margarine — 3 tablespoons

Pink colouring — 3 drops

Method: beat together to make a fudge.

Tom's Tip — Practise Your 'Layers'

What slices have in common is not the flour, but the principle of 'layering' the ingredients — layers of either shortbread, fillings or icings.

French Vanilla Slice

Wow, as if Vanilla Slice wasn't enough of a challenge...now you've gone this far, here's the French Vanilla Slice, which is really a carry-on from our Vanilla Slice. The layerings are:

• Pastry

• Custard which is quite creamy

• A layer of fresh cream

• Pastry again

• Chocolate icing

There's quite a bit of work in the French Vanilla Slice, but the result is quite beautiful. We do the pattern on the top. We put the chocolate on while the icing is soft and warm, and then it sets. Chris Brine has been doing it for so long she does it automatically.

Variation:

To make French Vanilla Slice — follow steps 1–5 of Vanilla Slice recipe. Level custard out. Allow to cool. Then add 300ml of whipped cream, level out cream, then add top pastry sheet (smooth side up).

Topping:

Cocoa powder — 1 tablespoon

Soft margarine — 4 tablespoons

Icing sugar — 1 cup

Method: beat together to make a fudge and spread it over the top.

Peppermint Slice

This is a recipe for Peppermint Slice which we have recently improvised by putting in orange juice instead of milk, and orange flavouring instead of peppermint. I think I'll call that the Sunraysia Slice.

(But for a crazier slice, use brandy essence, rum essence or anything else you fancy.)

Baking time: 12–15 minutes

Oven temperature: 200°C

Base:

Plain flour — 2 cups

Baking powder — 3 teaspoons

Desiccated coconut — $1^3/_4$ cups

Castor sugar — $^3/_4$ cups

Margarine — $1^1/_4$ cups

Filling:

Lard or dripping or supafry (solidified oil) — 100g or $^1/_2$ cup

Peppermint essence (use eye dropper) — 5 ml

Green colouring — 2 drops

Milk — $\frac{1}{4}$ cup

Icing sugar — $3\frac{1}{2}$ cups

Topping:

One cup or 250g melted chocolate

Method for the base:

1. Pre-heat oven to 200°C.

2. Mix all base-ingredients together until it resembles a shortbread mix.

3. Spread out on a greased slice tray using your fingertips.

4. Bake in oven at 200°C for approximately 12–15 minutes or until golden brown.

5. Allow to cool.

Method for the filling:

1. Heat fat until melted. Not too hot (in saucepan).

2. Mix together milk, essence and colour (in a cup).

3. Place icing sugar in mixing bowl.

4. Add milk mixtures to hot fat (not too hot) quickly and carefully.

5. Then add to icing sugar.

6. Mix together until smooth.

7. Quickly spread over slice base (as it will set fast).

8. Allow to set.

Method for topping:

1. Melt chocolate in microwave (see 'How To Melt Chocolate' on page 20).

2. Pour/spread over filling and mark and cut before chocolate sets to hard.

Tuscany Slice

We really should have called this one 'Barossa Slice' to make it sound Aussie, but a pre-mix company had that name registered. So we called it Tuscany Slice after the Tuscany Valley where they grow a lot of grapes. This slice is full of dried fruit, which is, of course, a grape product.

Base Ingredients:

Butter (softened) — $1\frac{1}{4}$ cups

Brown sugar — 1 cup tightly packed

Plain flour — 2 cups

Mix together base ingredients and spread over greased slice tray base evenly, then bake at 160°C for 20 minutes until light brown.

Method for base:

1.   Pre-heat oven.

2.   Bake base at 160°C.

3.   Allow to cool.

Topping Ingredients:

Eggs — 3 @ 65g

Brown sugar — $\frac{3}{4}$ cup

Vanilla essence — 1 teaspoon

Plain flour — 1 tablespoon

Baking powder — 1 teaspoon

Coconut shredded — $2\frac{1}{3}$ cups

Fruit mince — $1\frac{1}{2}$ cups

Method for topping:

1.   Combine egg, sugar, vanilla and fruit mince.

2.   Mix together in separate bowl: flour, baking powder, coconut.

3.   Combine the two mixtures and mix together.

4.   Spread over cooled base.

5.   Bake in oven at 160°C for 30 minutes.

Plain Scone (Lemonade Scone), Savoury Scones, Wasp Nests, Fetta Damper/Dan Kelly Damper, Date Scones, Pumpkin Scones, Cheese and Herb Scones

sconed!

Scones are easy to make and they're beautiful. A scone is very short eating; you bite straight through it. Where bread has a bit of strength and elasticity, with scones there's none of that. So it's not like 'bread', even though it is probably in the bread family. It's more like soda bread and damper. It's sconey — short and easy.

You can do many different fillings, as long as you do a good job with the foundation, which is the base scone recipe. You can do Cheese Scones, Savoury Scones, Pumpkin Scones, and you can have different fillings in all of them.

Again, a scone comes back to the foundation; you've got to have good flour. Again it's the preparation that makes the difference. And the weighing (or the scaling) of the ingredients.

In our bakehouse, everything is weighed with precision. A lot of bakeries don't do exact weights. They'll do a 'handful' of this and a 'handful' of that, and that's okay too, even though it's inconsistent. However, we weigh everything because everyone has got different size hands.

I go to the trouble of giving other bakers' scones the 'taste test'. Sometimes I buy one and it tastes terrible because they've put in too much baking powder.

Scones haven't got a long shelf life, but they do have a better-than-average freezer life. Make up a batch of scones and put them in the freezer and bake them off when you've got people over for afternoon tea. Or, bake them off, put them in the freezer, and stick them in the microwave and just warm them up when people come. You can actually put them in the oven frozen and they will bake out. But you're best to leave them out for half an hour so they come back to room temperature before you bake them. And, honestly, your guests will think you are unbelievable, because they'll have scones that taste absolutely fresh.

Scone dough is a wet dough. It's not tight dough, it's slack. You've got to use flour and a scraper — pick it up, drop it down. In that respect, it's very similar to damper. We use the same flour for all our scones, but we don't work it much. It's often mixed with milk, and as soon as the flour is absorbed, we stop the mixing.

One important tip is don't over-work scone dough, because the more you work it, the tougher the dough gets. You've got to treat scone doughs a little bit carefully, whereas the idea with bread dough is to work it to make it stronger.

Once you've got your basic scone recipe right, you can add many things to scones. You can make Pumpkin Scones or Cheese and Chive Scones, then you might even think, "I love prunes, so I'll make some prune scones". As long as the prunes aren't too wet, you will succeed.

Plain Scone (Lemonade Scone)

The Plain Scone is really a 'lemonade scone'. At the Beechworth Bakery, we use real lemonade, although I must admit you can just use cheap lemonade if you like. Nobody's going to pick the difference after it's been cooked.

Makes 16

Oven temperature: 175°C

Baking time: 15–18 minutes

Ingredients:

Plain flour — $6^1/_2$ cups

Baking powder — $3^1/_2$ tablespoons

Salt — 2 teaspoons

Castor sugar — $^1/_2$ cup

Lemonade — $1^3/_4$ cups or 375ml

Cream — $1^3/_4$ cups

Method:

1.   Pre-heat oven to 175°C.

2.   Mix together dry ingredients in a large bowl.

3.   Add lemonade and cream.

4.   Knead together to form a soft dough. Don't over-knead.

5.   Turn out into slightly floured board.

6.   Roll out to $2^1/_2$cm thick (30cm by 30cm).

7.   Cut 16 squares.

8.   Place on greased oven tray.

9.   Brush top with milk,

10. Bake at 175°C for 15–18 minutes.

Savoury Scones

The Savoury Scone is like a Wasp Nest Scone without the curry. We sell heaps of Savoury Scones.

You can just have cheese and onion, or you can change to ricotta cheese and spinach. And if you don't like bacon, you can have a substitute or you can just leave it out. So again, with this scone, as long as you've got the basic recipe right, you can do many different kinds of fillings.

For Mediterranean scones add olives, sundried tomato, capsicum, salami with a bit of olive oil, chopped up together with scone mix.

Makes: 16–18

Preparation time: 15 minutes

Baking time: 15–18 minutes

Oven temperature: 180°C–190°C

Ingredients:

Plain flour — 3 cups

Margarine — $1/4$ cup

Castor sugar — $1/4$ cup

Salt — 1 teaspoon

Baking powder — $1 1/4$ tablespoons

Milk — $1 1/4$ cups

Cheese, grated, tasty — 2 cups, firmly packed

Diced bacon — 1 cup firmly packed

Onion chopped — 1 cup

Eggs — 2 @ 55g

Parsley flakes — 2 teaspoons

Tom's Tip — Gently, Gently...

If you overwork your scones, they get too tough. The idea with scone dough is to mix it gently, treat it gently.

Method:

1. Pre-heat oven to 180°C–190°C.

2. Mix together flour, margarine, sugar, salt and baking powder (rub margarine through dry ingredients).

3. Mix in milk to form a soft dough.

4. Allow 10 minutes for dough to rest.

5. Roll out to 30cm by 24cm, approximately $^3/_4$cm thick.

6. In a bowl, mix cheese, onion, bacon, eggs and parsley.

7. Spread evenly over dough.

8. Roll up like a log, then using a bread knife, cut slices approximately 3cm thick.

9. Place on greased baking tray, allowing room for each to spread, and bake for approximately 15–18 minutes at 180°C–190°C.

10. Butter them and eat them while they're hot — with a slice of cheese, there's nothing like them!

Wasp Nests

We are very famous for our Wasp Nests, made from a Savoury Scone recipe which we sheet through our computerised dough sheeter — but you'd use a rolling pin at home for this task.

First, you roll it out, then you put in a filling of cheese, bacon, fresh onions, eggs and curry; then you scroll it up like a Coffee Scroll.

They're really a 'Pinwheel Curry Scone', but we call them Wasp Nests because they've got a bit of a sting.

Variation:

Instead of parsley, add mixed herbs (2 teaspoons), curry powder (1 tablespoon) and a thin slice of tomato on top before baking.

Fetta Damper/Dan Kelly Damper

Makes 1 loaf

Preparation time: 20 minutes

Baking time: 35–40 minutes

Oven temperature: 190°C

Ingredients:

Group 1

Plain flour — 3 cups

Margarine — 2 tablespoons

Salt — $1/4$ teaspoon

Baking Powder — 1 tablespoon + 1 teaspoon

Group 2

Milk — $1/3$ cup

Water — $1/2$ cup

Group 3

Fetta cheese (crumbled pea size) — 85g to 100g or $3/4$ cup

Grated tasty cheese — $1/2$ cup lightly packed

Spinach/Silverbeet (torn up) — $3/4$ cup lightly packed

Method:

1. Pre-heat oven 190°C.
2. Place group 1 in a bowl and rub margarine with flour, salt and baking powder.
3. Add group 2, as this comes together to form a dough add group 3.
4. Mix/knead to form a dough for 1 or 2 minutes, then roll up to form a log or a cigar shape.
5. Place on a baking tray then cut down centre around 2cm deep.
6. Dust with flour lightly and bake.

Date Scone

Date Scones are another of my favourites, and everybody else's too I think, judging by the number that we sell. You can't beat a warm date scone with a bit of butter.

Makes: 18

Preparation time: 18 minutes

Baking time: 15–18 minutes

Oven temperature: 180°C–190°C

Ingredients:

Plain flour — 6 cups

Margarine — $^3/_4$ cup

Castor sugar — $^1/_2$ cup

Salt — 2 teaspoons

Baking powder — $2^1/_2$ tablespoons

Milk — $2^1/_2$ cups

Dates (pitted and finely chopped) — $1^1/_2$ cups

Method:

1. Pre-heat to 180°C–190°C.

2. Mix together flour, sugar, salt, baking powder. Rub margarine through.

3. Mix in milk to form a soft dough. Do not over mix.

4. Mix through dates.

5. Allow to rest for 10 minutes.

6. Roll out on lightly floured bench top/board, 20cm by 40cm ($2^1/_2$cm thick). Cut squares 6cm x 6cm.

7. Brush top with milk.

8. Place on greased tray allowing room to spread. Bake at 200°C for 15–18 minutes.

Pumpkin Scone

A lot of people who don't like eating pumpkin in general, love our nutty-flavoured pumpkin scones, because they're a bit sweet.

Makes: 16

Preparation time: 15 minutes

Baking time: 15–18 minutes

Oven temperature: 175°C

Ingredients:

Plain flour — 6 cups

Margarine — $^3/_4$ cup

Castor sugar — $^1/_2$ cup

Salt — 2 teaspoons

Baking powder — $2^1/_2$ tablespoons

Milk — $1^1/_2$ cups

Pumpkin (pre-cooked, cooled, drained and lightly mashed) — $1^1/_2$ cups or 400g)

Nutmeg — 1 teaspoon

Method:

1. Pre-heat oven at 175°C.

2. Mix together flour, sugar, nutmeg, salt, baking powder. Rub margarine through.

3. Mix in pumpkin and milk until it forms a soft dough. Do not over-mix.

4. Roll out to $2^1/_2$cm thick square (30cm x 30cm).

5. Cut 16 squares.

6. Place on greased tray allowing room for each to spread.

7. Brush top with milk and bake at 175°C for 15–18 minutes.

Variation:

1. Pumpkin can be roasted in the skin then peeled and mashed to give extra flavour.

2. Add $^1/_2$ cup of grated cheese to make pumpkin and cheese scones.

3. Mixed herbs, cracked pepper.

4. Add cream in place of milk if you like it rich.

Cheese and Herb Scones

Cheese and Herb Scones are for all the cheese freaks out there. You know the type of people I mean. They get a cheese roll, cut it through the middle and add camembert cheese. Or they cover a cheese flavoured Share & Tear with havarti, stick it in the microwave for 30 seconds so it comes out all runny. Well, the Cheese & Herb Scones are ideal for the cheese-on-cheese people.

Makes: 18

Preparation time: 15 minutes

Baking time: 15–18 minutes

Oven temperature: 180°C–190°C

Ingredients:

Plain flour — 6 cups

Margarine — $^3/_4$ cup

Castor sugar — $^1/_2$ cup

Salt — 2 teaspoons

Baking powder — $2^1/_2$ tablespoons

Milk — $2^1/_2$ cups

Grated cheese — 2 cups (250g)

Mixed herbs — 1 tablespoon

Method:

1. Pre-heat to 180°C–190°C.

2. Mix together flour, sugar, salt, baking powder. Rub margarine through.

3. Mix in milk to form a soft dough. Do not over-mix.

4. Mix in two cups of grated cheese and mixed herbs.

5. Allow to rest for 10 minutes.

6. Roll out on lightly floured bench top/board, 20cm by 40cm ($2^1/_2$cm thick). Cut squares 6cm x 6cm.

7. Brush top with milk.

8. Place on greased tray allowing room to spread. Bake at 200°C for 15–18 minutes.

Basic Sweet Muffins (Apple Muffins, Raspberry Muffins, Blueberry Muffins), Basic Savoury Muffins (or Loaf).

muffins are great

What we need out of every recipe book is a success. Next to biscuits and scones, I would rate muffins as the easiest products in this book to make. So I suggest you do a muffin and you'll get a success. A muffin is pretty well foolproof. Your confidence as a cook will rise as you make these beautiful muffins, then you can go on to greater things.

It's your stepping stone to glory. We do a Morning Glory muffin.

We do two basic doughs: (1) a basic sweet muffin mix and (2) a savoury mix, and we make every variation out of those two.

From the basic sweet dough we make raspberry, blueberry, pineapple, cinnamon and rhubarb muffin variations. And from the savoury we make cream cheese, corn, spinach, fetta, on and on and on. Most of our muffins are pulled straight out of the oven and served oven-finished.

The sky's the limit. You don't have to be that creative and you can get some really different muffins. Muffins are universal, for vegetarians and meat lovers, and from breakfast to midnight. Muffins are an incredible after-school snack and we also do a good muffin breakfast.

Blueberry Muffins, Apple Muffins, Apple and Cinnamon Muffins, Sweet and Savoury Muffins...again the mind just boggles with what you can do with just one recipe. So long as you've got the base right, you can add this and add that, and you've got it!

Basic Sweet Muffins

Apple Muffins, Raspberry Muffins, Blueberry Muffins

When the muffins are cold, make some jelly up — lime, raspberry, etc. Dip in your muffins while the jelly is still warm, then roll them in the coconut and you've got a muffin lamington.

You can use stale ones or fresh ones, though slightly stale ones are better, because they don't fall apart in the jelly. Or, if they're fresh, freeze them first, so they don't fall apart when you dip them.

Makes: 16–18 large muffins

Oven temperature: 180°C

Baking time: 25–30 minutes

Ingredients:

Plain flour — $3\frac{1}{2}$ cups

Castor sugar — 1 cup

Baking powder — $1\frac{1}{4}$ tablespoons

Salt — $1\frac{1}{2}$ teaspoon

Margarine — $\frac{1}{2}$ cup

Milk — $1\frac{1}{2}$ cup

Egg — 4 @ 50g

Method:

1. Pre-heat oven to 180°C.

2. Rub together flour, sugar, baking powder, salt and margarine.

3. Mix together milk and eggs.

4. Add the two groups together and mix until all dry ingredients are moistened. Do not over-mix.

5. Fold through fruit.

6. Drop into greased muffin tins.

7. Bake in oven for 25–30 minutes at 180°C.

8. Allow to cool, then dust with icing sugar.

Variations:

Instead of fruit, add 3 tablespoons of cocoa powder with the flour to make chocolate muffins. Then add $1\frac{1}{2}$ cup of chocolate chips, it's up to you.

Fruit options:

*   Apple (tinned) — $1\frac{1}{2}$ cup (400g)

*   Raspberries — 2 cups (300g)

*   Blueberries — 2 cups

*   Cinnamon and mixed spice — to taste

Basic Savoury Muffins (or Loaf)

You can make two large muffins or a dozen-and-a-half small muffins out of the following muffin mix. Most people don't make a Muffin Loaf, but I think they are terrific.

Matthew discovered the idea while making up these recipes. When he made up the total mix, he cut it in half and made nine muffins, and (because 18 muffins were too much for his family to eat) he took the rest of the dough and made a Muffin Loaf. When it had cooled down he sliced it and made sandwiches and his wife, Sharron, ate them and then gave him a big kiss for his efforts.

To make 16–18 large muffins or 2 muffin loaves

Preparation time: 15 minutes

Baking time: 20 minutes

Oven temperature: 160°C

Group 1

Milk — $1^1/_2$ cups

Oil — $^1/_4$ cup

Grated cheese — $2^1/_3$ cups (soft packed)

Parmesan cheese — $^3/_4$ cup

Frozen spinach (fine chopped/thawed) or zucchini — $^3/_4$ cup

Chilli sauce — 1 tablespoon

Eggs — 3 @ 55g

Group 2

Plain flour — $3^1/_2$ cups

Baking powder — 1 tablespoon

Salt — 1 teaspoon

Tom's Tip — If You're Inexperience Around A Kitchen

What we need out of every recipe book is a success. Next to biscuits and scones, I would rate muffins as the easiest product in this book to make. So I suggest you do a muffin and you'll get a success.

Method:

1. Pre-heat oven at 160°C.

2. Mix group 1.

3. Sift group 2.

4. Combines groups 1 and 2 to form a batter. Do not over-mix.

5. Place mix in greased muffin tins or two large loaf tins and bake at 160°C for 20 minutes or for loaf tin approximately 40 minutes, depending on the size of tins.

6. Allow to cool.

Variation:

Use grated zucchini instead of spinach. Mix in $1/2$ tablespoon of mixed herbs.

Anzac Biscuits, Christmas Shortbread, Ginger Crunch, Afghans, Choc Chip, Jam Drops, Yo Yos, Shortbread, Shortbread Recipe for Kids!

American cookies are chewier. They take them out of the oven earlier and their make-up is a little bit different than in Australia. We consider their cookies a little unbaked. Americans also put in more sugar and fat.

Although scones and muffins are easy to make, I'd say biscuits are even easier, which means they are the easiest things to make in this recipe book. Biscuit-making is a great project for involving the kids. We can all do Anzac Biscuits. Come on, I'm sure you can!

Biscuits are wonderful. I love our Choc Chips, I love our Afghans. I love Iced Vovos. And I love Arnott's Monte Carlo biscuits. I'll often have one when I'm in the Golden Wing lounges. However, we don't usually buy supermarket biscuits for our own home, mainly because if we did, the kids would probably eat them straight away. But who needs to buy biscuits when there's the Beechworth Bakery? We always have biscuits at home. If you were here you could share these Afghans with me — I love our biscuits.

Biscuit flour is different to bread and cake flour. The wheat is not as strong and they have a longer shelf life. From biscuit flour you can make a heck of a range: savoury bites, sweet biscuits, wafers, lemon biscuits, chewy biscuits, crisp biscuits, some with baking powder, some without. And then come the fillings — nuts, chocolate, raspberry jam, dried fruits — and again it's unlimited.

The sky's the limit, if your heart's in it.

I always wanted to 'invent' a biscuit and name it.

I said to my staff, "Look at these names. Iced Vovos. Tim Tams. What incredible names! We've got to come up with one. If you can name something 'Vovo', you can call anything, anything!"

But I haven't come up with one — not yet — although I know I've got to.

And I will.

Anzac Biscuits

Talking about great names, I love a fresh Anzac Biscuit. I don't know why it is, but I always think about those fellas at Gallipoli every time I eat one.

I don't have sad thoughts. I just think that the biscuit I'm eating must have a good Anzac story to get a name like that. I got told at school it was because eggs were impossible to get in the city during the war so they invented a biscuit that didn't require eggs.

Makes: 24

Preparation time: 10 minutes

Baking time: 15–18 minutes

Oven temperature: 160°C

Ingredients:

Rolled oats — 2 cups

Sugar — $^1/_2$ cup

Plain flour — $^3/_4$ cup

Golden Syrup — 1 tablespoon

Bicarb soda — 1 teaspoon

Hot water — 2 tablespoons

Butter (softened) — $^1/_2$ cup

Method:

1. Set oven at 160°C.

2. Mix oats, sugar, flour, golden syrup and butter.

3. In a separate cup, mix soda and hot water. While frothing, add to other ingredients, mix thoroughly.

4. Drop tablespoonfuls of mix onto greased tray. Allow room for mixture to spread.

5. Bake at 160°C for 15–18 minutes or until golden brown.

6. Allow to cool on tray/place on cake wire.

Christmas Shortbread

Preparation time: 20 minutes

Baking time: 15–18 minutes

Oven temperature: 190°C–200°C

Tom's Tip

This shortbread is crumbly as it is so rich and short. Try rolling out between 2 thick plastic sheets.

Ingredients:

Group 1

Castor sugar — $1\frac{1}{2}$ cups

Butter — 1 x 500g block

Group 2

Plain flour — $4\frac{1}{3}$ cups

Rice flour — $\frac{1}{2}$ cup

Salt — 1 teaspoon

Method:

1. Cream group 1 together in bowl with a blender until smooth.

2. Dry mix group 2 together, add to group 1 and mix by hand till it comes together to form a shortbread.

3. Roll out 1cm thick, cut shapes to suit; or in the bakehouse we roll out one large sheet, place it on a baking tray and mark, not cut, just mark out squares.

4. Prick with a fork, lightly brush with water and then sprinkle sugar on top.

5. Cook at 190°C–200°C until pastry is just coloured around the edge, let it cool on a tray, then remove and snap into biscuits along marked lines.

Ginger Crunch

Some people don't like ginger, but everybody loves a Ginger Crush biscuit — especially kids when they drink their milk, or adults when they drink their tea or coffee.

Makes: 20

Baking time: 12–15 minutes

Oven temperature: 170°C

Ingredients:

Butter — $\frac{3}{4}$ cup

Castor sugar — 1 cup

Golden Syrup — $\frac{1}{4}$ cup

Baking powder — 2 teaspoons

Ginger — 2 teaspoons

Plain flour — 2¹/₂ cups

Sultanas — 1 cup

Method:

1.   Pre-heat over to 170°C

2.   Cream together butter, sugar, Golden Syrup, baking powder and ginger. Mix really well.

3.   Combine flour and sultanas with other ingredients.

4.   Spoon out with soup spoon onto two greased trays and allow room to spread.

5.   Bake for 12–15 minutes at 170°C.

6.   Allow to cool on trays.

Tom's Tip—The Sugar

Although there is a fair difference in the grades of sugar — castor, icing, IA, raw and brown — generally speaking, there is no significant quality difference between generic brands and name brands.

Afghans

I love our Afghan biscuits. I'm eating one now.

Makes: 20

Baking time: 12–15 minutes

Oven temperature: 180°C

Ingredients:

Butter — 1¹/₄ cup

Castor sugar — 1¹/₃ cups

Egg — 1 x 50g

Plain flour — 2¹/₃ cups

Cocoa powder — ¹/₄ cup

Baking powder — 3 teaspoons

Cornflakes — $2^3/_4$ cups

Melted chocolate

Method:

1. Pre-heat oven at 180°C.

2. Cream together softened butter and sugar.

3. Slowly add egg.

4. Mix flour, cocoa powder and baking powder together.

5. Add to butter and sugar mixture and mix through.

6. Then fold in cornflakes, making sure not to overmix.

7. Spoon onto greased baking tray, allow room to sprea.

8. Bake at 180°C for 12–15 minutes.

9. Coat in melted chocolate after cooled (melt in microwave). See page 20.

Choc Chip

The Chocolate Chip Biscuit is one of the world's best sellers today, yet it was created by accident in 1933.

It was supposed to be a biscuit with the chocolate evenly spread throughout, and when they were making it they expected the chocolate to melt through. They didn't know that chocolate has a different melting point to the cooking temperature of a biscuit. Instead, the chocolate stayed in little chips, and because it tasted so great, they left the recipe that way.

Butter also has a different melting point. A lot of people don't realise that.

Makes: 20

Baking time: 12–15 minutes

Oven temperature: 180°C–190°C

Ingredients:

Castor sugar — $1^1/_8$ cup

Butter (soft) — $^1/_2$ cup

Eggs — 50g x 2

Plain flour — 2$^2/_3$ cups

Baking powder — 1 tablespoon

Small chocolate chips — $^3/_4$ cup

Method:

1. Pre-heat oven at 180°C.

2. Cream butter and sugar until light and fluffy.

3. Add 1 egg, cream into mix.

4. Add next egg, cream into mix until light and fluffy.

5. Sieve flours and baking powder together.

6. Fold flour mix into butter and egg/sugar mixture.

7. Blend in chocolate chips, do not over mix.

8. Place on greased baking tray, allow room to spread.

9. Bake at 180°C–190°C. 12–15 minutes, or until golden brown.

Jam Drops

Jam Drops are ideal for afternoon teas. When someone drops in for a cup of tea or coffee, you might say, "Would you like a biscuit with that, Auntie Dolly?"

She'll say, "Yes". You'll give her a couple of Jam Drops. And she'll be real nice for the rest of the afternoon.

Makes: 20

Baking time: 12–15 minutes

Oven temperature: 180°C–190°C

Ingredients:

Castor sugar — 1$^1/_8$ cup

Butter — $^1/_2$ cup

Eggs — 50g x 2

Plain flour — 2$^2/_3$ cups

Baking powder — 1 tablespoon

Vanilla essence — 2 teaspoons

Jam

Method:

1. Pre-heat oven to 180°C.

2. Cream butter and sugar until light and fluffy.

3. Add 1 egg. Cream into mix.

4. Add next egg, cream into mix until light and fluffy.

5. Add vanilla essence.

6. In a separate bowl, sieve flour and baking powder together.

7. Fold flour into butter, egg and sugar mixture.

8. Use soup spoon to spoon onto greased tray. Allow room for each one to spread.

9. Make an indent in centre with your fingertip (not right through to tray).

10. Fill the indent with jam.

11. Bake at 180°C–190°C for 12–15 minutes or until golden brown.

12. Allow to cool on cake wire.

Yo Yos

Iced Vovos. There are more words like this than you'd think: Bobo, Toto, Dodo, Go Go, Ho Ho, No No, Jo Jo, Zo Zo, etc.

Anyway, here's a recipe for Yo Yos.

Makes approximately: 25 finished biscuits

Baking time: 15–18 minutes

Oven temperature: 160°C

Ingredients:

Butter (soft) — 1 cup

Icing sugar — $1/_3$ cup

Custard powder — $1/_3$ cup

Plain flour — $1^1/_4$ cups

Method:

1. Pre heat oven at 160°C.

2. Cream butter and sugar real well, until light and fluffy.

3. Dry mix custard powder and flour and add to cream mixture.

4. Scoop small size teaspoon size (approx 10g each), press down with fork, dip fork in hot water so as not to stick, you should get approximately 50 small biscuits.

5. Bake at 160°C for approximately 12–15 minutes or until lightly golden brown around edges.

6. Allow to cool.

7. Prepare icing.

8. Stick together two biscuits back to back with icing.

9. Make approximately 25 finished biscuits.

Tom's Tip—The Butter

When you're doing cake recipes, remember that butter melts at a different temperature to the batter, and (without warming) the butter won't go through the mix properly, which is a real hassle.

Icing for Yo Yos:

Beat together the following:

Icing sugar — $1\frac{1}{4}$ cups

Soft butter — $\frac{1}{3}$ cup

1 lemon juice and fine grated rind.

Shortbread

There are different shortbreads: there's the Scottish shortbread, which is crisp, and there are other varieties which are buttery. It's called shortbread because it's short eating, 'short' being the abbreviation of 'shortening'. Ours is a rich crumbly biscuit. It's a very Australianised shortbread.

I was making shortbread once during my apprenticeship when my boss Frank told me to put the sausage meat in the mixer.

I said, "Where did you say you wanted me to put the sausage meat?"

"I've told you, you silly dumb bastard. Stick it in the mixer," Frank yelled, forgetting that the shortbread was in the mixer. "Bloody put it in there."

So I put the sausage meat in with the shortbread and mixed them together. I then turned to Frank and weakly said, "Gee, it looks funny".

He was going to kill me.

As I was running around the room with him chasing me, I yelled, "But it was you who told me to put it in."

So there are obviously limits to innovation, and now that we have 'successfully identified' that meat and shortbread is a terrible combination — you'll know not to try it yourself.

Makes approximately 32 biscuits

Baking time: 12 minutes

Oven temperature: 190°C–200°C

Tom's Tip—Use Airtight Containers

Keep your biscuits in an airtight container and you will get weeks and weeks out of them.

Ingredients:

Group 1

Castor sugar — 1 cup

Butter (softened) — $1\frac{1}{3}$ cups

Rice flour — $\frac{1}{4}$ cup

Plain flour — 1 cup

Group 2

Egg — 1 @ 55g

Group 3

Plain flour — 2 cups

Baking powder — $\frac{1}{4}$ teaspoon

Salt — $\frac{1}{4}$ teaspoon

Method:

1. Pre-heat oven at 190°C.

2. Mix group 1 until smooth.

3. Add group 2 and mix until soft.

4. Dry mix group 3. Add to form a smooth dough.

5. Roll into fat log shape (40cm long). Place in freezer for $^1/_2$ hour to form solid log. Slice rings, 1cm thick off log, to make round biscuits.

6. Place on greased tray.

7. Bake in oven for 12 minutes at 190°C–200°C or until pale in colour.

8. Allow to cool.

Variations:

Add $^1/_3$ cup cocoa powder, sieve through with flour to step 2 (to make chocolate shortbread) or add 1 cup coconut to step 2 for coconut shortbread.

Tom's Tip—Shortbread Mix

You will be using shortbread a lot in desserts, so have a mix on hand in the fridge ready to go!

Shortbread Recipe For The Kids!

Method:

1. Make one mix of shortbread from recipe.

2. Roll out to $1^1/_2$cm thick.

3. Cut into shapes, such as shortbread men, squares or circles. You could also use cookie cutters — be creative.

4. Bake at 180°C for 10–12 minutes or until light golden colour around edges.

5. Allow to cool — then decorate.

Suggestion: Ice with icing or chocolate, then add coconut, jam, currants, sultanas, 100s & 1000s, or lollies.

Icing for Shortbread

Ingredients:

Icing sugar (sifted) —1$^1/_2$ cups

Egg white — 1x 55g egg white

Lemon juice —$^1/_2$ teaspoon

Method:

1. Beat egg white until light and fluffy.

2. Sift icing sugar.

3. Add 1 cup of icing sugar to egg white, mix in.

4. Add lemon juice and mix in all icing sugar.

5. If mix is to wet, add more icing sugar, if mix is to dry, add more lemon juice. Make icing consistency to suit for dipping, spreading or piping.

Eclairs, Bavarian Rings and Cream Puffs, Pecan Pie, Neenish Tarts, Fruit Mince Tarts, Fruit Pies (Apple, Blueberry, Apricot, Apple and Rhubarb, Apple and Sultana, Blueberry and Apple, Quince and Apple and Cinnamon), Lemon Meringue Pie, Snickerdoodles, Fruit Squares, Fruit Eccles/Fruit Strudel/Squares, Croissants, Christmas Pudding.

just desserts

Pastry has been around for a long, long time in a multitude of different forms. Pastry was known before the Roman times and was a real feature of medieval cooking. It's a very European thing.

Today, very sophisticated variations of pastry have been an essential part of the development of the Western world. Pastry has evolved dramatically with Danish pastry, croissant pastry and filo pastry. But here in Australia we use a lot of sheet pastry — which we call puff or flaky pastry.

There is no revolutionary new method for doing pastry.

With everything else you can get away with a little bit of this and a little bit of that,

but with pastry you really can't.

You've got to be careful.

It's probably easier to go to the supermarket and buy it ready-rolled from the freezer.

There is a science to pastry. You don't have the flexibility to improvise with pastry as you do with other lines. Everybody adapts and changes recipes, but pastry doesn't lend itself to modification. You've got to be a bit careful. There are a lot of easier products to make, because with pastry — if you want the puff, if you want the lift — you've got to do the laminations. There's no short cut.

Also, your room should be cool, not hot. And you've got to be prepared to get flour all over the place. But don't worry about it. You don't have to be a 'real' chef. In today's society, people want it easy-made and...supermarkets sell everything frozen.

But to master the art of pastry-making, you've got to persevere and practise. It's worth the perseverance. Pastry is a skill that improves with repetition. You get to feel and understand why something didn't work. You learn to get it perfect by doing it over and over and over again.

I love making pastry.

I'm good at making pastry.

I enjoy doing puff pastry, strudel pastry, turnover pastry.

I find it very peaceful.

I get a real buzz out of making pastry.

To get good Danish and good croissants, you must have your mind on the job. You've got to concentrate to keep the job moving through, plus you need to keep it cool...

All our pastries are done with vegetable shortening, which is vegetable margarine. It's a little bit harder but you do get a clean bite when you eat. There is no oily after-taste, none at all.

We do a three-quarter pastry — three quarters of it is margarine, so it's very rich. If there's 10kg of flour there'll be 7.5kg of margarine, and we fold it in to get that lamination which gives you the great pastry. Laminations are when you fold one layer over the top of another, something like 'bookfolds' — and each fold has got its name. Lyn, Jenny, Tinna, Keith, Carol, Ian...or something like that, when you're not thinking straight.

When you are thinking straight, remember the old rule — that good ingredients are the foundation for excellent pastry. If you want the best product, you need good foundations.

The Shortbread Dough

We do a very Australianised shortbread, and we also use it as the base for our Apple Slice, Apple Pie, Pecan Pie, Snickerdoodles, Apple Cake base, Blueberry Pies, etc.

And the thing is — when you do a shortbread at home you have got the basis for doing so many sweetgoods. You can mix the pastry, wrap it in plastic and put it in the fridge, and you can pull it out next week or next month. Get it back to room temperature, roll it out, and make an Apricot Pie.

Next week make a Blueberry Pie.

The week after, do some Snickerdoodles or a Pecan Pie.

That shortbread base is incredible.

It is one of the most versatile products that we have in the bakehouse!

Eclairs, Bavarian Rings and Cream Puffs

The greatest thing is to see the look on people's faces when they bite into an Eclair — especially when they get cream on their nose. An Eclair would have to be right up there with the top of my favourites.

I often get an Eclair and think, "I'll be good; I'll only eat half".

And I eat half and think, "I've been good, so I'll eat the other half."

Choux ('Shoe') paste is a French word. And once you get the choux paste right you can do many, many things. Choux paste is an oddity; it is half-cooked before baking, with high egg and water content. You beat it in over the stove and it's quite different. It's getting that consistency right —

you go too slack

    and you're Eclairs are flat

        go too tight

           and they don't steam up right:

                they're dead.

You must have the right consistency to generates the steam that puffs them up and gives them that moist interior.

And then you fill them either with continental custard or a beautiful banana custard. The main ones we sell are our fresh cream with chocolate fondant (an icing) on top.

You cannot beat our Eclairs.

They are absolutely superb.

They're orgasmic.

They are just divine.

They're bloody beautiful.

Again you can put savoury fillers in them, but if you do that, remember not to put chocolate fondant on the top!

We do our Banana Eclairs a bit curved with banana custard in them, and then we pour a yellow fondant on the top and we dribble a little bit of chocolate over it. Eclairs deliver a real lot without a real lot of work.

Bavarian Cream Rings are another variation of the Eclair. We call them Bavarian Rings, but the real name is 'Paris Brest'. Again we change and Australianise, not that Australians have anything against Paris breasts.

Preparation time: 30 minutes

Baking time: 35 minutes

Oven temperature: 220°C

Group 1

Water — 1 cup

Butter — $\frac{1}{2}$ cup

Group 2

Plain flour — 1 cup

Group 3

Eggs — 3 x 55g

Method:

1. Pre-heat oven at 220°C.

2. Sift flour.

3. Place group 1 in saucepan and heat it on the stove — melt butter, bring to a rolling boil.

4. Remove from heat. As it is still boiling add group 2 and mix in well until mixture leaves the sides of the pot and is smooth.

5. Allow to cool for 5 minutes.

6. Place mix in bowl. Using electric mixer on high, mix in one egg at a time.

7. Beat until mixture is glassy and smooth.

8. Wet with water 2 oven trays.

9. Place mix in piping bag with a 2cm nozzle.

To make Chocolate Eclairs:

1. Pipe mix 10cm long on tray.

2. Place in oven at 220°C for 10 minutes. Then turn heat down to 180°C for 25 minutes.

3. Cool on wire after baking.

4. Dip top in melted chocolate or dust with icing sugar. Cut in half and fill with fresh, whipped cream.

To make Bavarian Rings:

1. Pipe rings on tray — make them so you could fit a 10 cent coin in the centre hole.

2. Place in oven and bake at 220°C for 10 minutes. Turn heat down to 180°C for 25 minutes.

3. Cool on wire after baking.

4. Prepare recipe from Lemon Meringue Pie Filling recipe page without group 3, follow steps 1–5.

5. When filling is cool, fold in 300ml of whipped cream.

7. Dip top of ring in chocolate or dust with icing sugar.

8. Cut in half and fill with custard cream filling.

For something different: Add two teaspoons of coffee flavouring to filling.

To make Cream Puffs:

1. Pipe mix the size of a walnut on to trays.

2. Place in oven and bake at 220°C for 10 minutes.

3. Turn heat down to 180°C for 25 minutes.

4. Cool on wire.

5. Fill with fresh whipped cream or Bavarian filling (try it with bananas and cream).

6. Dust with icing sugar.

Pecan Pie

You won't find many recipes for Pecan Pie in the old cook books, because they were so expensive in the old days people used to eat walnuts instead.

Then the farmers ripped out all their walnut trees, put in pecans which were more profitable, and ironically the price of pecans has come down — while the price of walnuts is up!

Makes one

Baking time: 18–24 minutes

Oven temperature: 160°C

Pecan pie base:

1. Use half of shortbread recipe from previous Biscuits section, steps 1–4.

2. Roll out and line 20cm flan tin.

3. Blind bake base lightly (i.e. 'Blind bake' - place a piece of tin foil in flan tin on top of shortbread and fill with dry rice or lentils and bake in oven 200°C to make a pre-baked shell).

Pecan pie-filling ingredients:

Brown sugar — $^1/_4$ cup

Golden Syrup — $^1/_4$ cup

Margarine — $^1/_4$ cup

Egg — 1 @ 65g

Plain flour — 3 tablespoons

Baking powder - $^1/_2$ teaspoon

Coconut - $1^1/_2$ cups

Pecan nuts (broken) - $1^1/_2$ cups

Castor sugar — 1 teaspoon

Pecan nuts (for top of pie) — $^3/_4$ cup (250g pecan nuts, total)

Method:

1. Pre-heat oven at 160°C.

2. Sieve together, white flour, baking powder.

3. Mix in coconut, castor sugar, broken pieces of pecan nuts.

4. Melt your margarine, Golden Syrup and brown sugar, keep stirring, don't let it burn.

5. Add to dry ingredients. Mix together.

6. Add egg, mix in,

7. Place filling in pre-baked shortbread flan and top with pecan nuts and bake at approximately 18-24 minutes at 160°C. Allow to cool.

Neenish Tarts

I won't eat Neenish Tarts because they are just too sweet, but some people just love them. They're full of a butter filling and definitely not a candidate for the Heart Foundation tick.

In some states Neenish Tarts are passionfruit and white. In others, they're white and chocolate.

Neenish Tarts are very English. Some people think ours is not a real Neenish because they haven't got a dob of jam in the bottom.

But in Victoria, and in our bakery, we do them pink and chocolate — half and half fondant on the top, full with butter cream — and that's 'Neenish' enough for us and our customers.

Tart Base — To Form a Shortbread Cup:

*   Prepare full batch of shortbread.

*   Roll out and cut to size to suit muffin tins.

*   Get your muffin tins, turn them upside down.

*   Lay shortbread disk over top of muffin tin bottom and mould to shape off tin base,

- Bake at 180°C for approximately 12 minutes until light golden colour. Allow to cool.
- Take shell off tin and add filling.

Filling:

Butter (softened) — $3/_4$cup

Condensed milk — $1/_2$ cup

Icing sugar — $1^1/_4$cups

Add some flavour to suit — vanilla, strawberry, raspberry, rum, etc.

Method:

1. Mix together. Beat until light and fluffy.
2. Fill shortbread bases.

Topping:

1. Allow to sit in refrigerator to set.
2. Top with melted chocolate and/or toasted coconut.

Fruit Mince Tarts

This is Auntie Dolly's favourite. And everybody's got an Auntie Dolly.

Preparation time: $1/_2$ hour

Oven temperature: 200°C

Baking time: 12–18 minutes

Prepare shortbread from shortbread recipe — steps 2–4.

Fruit mince filling:

1. Pre-heat oven to 200°C.
2. To every one cup of fruit mince add one tablespoon of rum or brandy.
3. Also add $1/_4$ cup of biscuit crumb, which adds flavour, and the crumb stops fruit from boiling in the oven.
4. Roll out the shortbread to 1cm thick and cut to desired size for tart tins and line base of greased tins.
5. Add prepared fillings taking care not to over-fill.
6. Place shortbread tops on tarts.

7. Prick tops with a fork several times.

8. Bake at 200°C for 12–18 minutes, depending on the size of the tarts, or until golden brown.

9. Dust with icing sugar when cool.

fruit Pies

Apple, Blueberry, Apricot, Apple and Rhubarb, Apple and Sultana, Blueberry and Apple, Quince and Apple and Cinnamon

We love our apples at the Beechworth Bakery, because they are grown just up the road at Stanley. (I also like to add a little bit of apple to blueberry pies.)

Tom's Tip—Apple Slice

Here's one of the tricks of doing Apple Slices at home. Pre-bake the sheet of shortbread a little — bake it only three-quarters, then let it cool down before you put the apple on it.

Next, put a sheet of raw shortbread on the top and bake it off, cool it and serve it — it's nice with yoghurt.

Pre-bake because all the apple weighing down doesn't let the base bake out. And often in home kitchens it probably wouldn't hurt you to pre-bake the base of the apple pie. You'll often find you'll bake the apple pie off and it looks beautiful on the top, but it's all raw underneath and really disappointing.

Baking time: 18–20 minutes

Oven temperature: 200°C

Shortbread:

• Prepare a full mix of shortbread from shortbread recipe for base of pie.

• Roll shortbread out 1cm thick to line 23cm pie plate and blind bake base at 200°C for 12–15 minutes or until shortbread is light golden brown.

Blind Baking:

Place a piece of tin foil in a pie dish on top of shortbread and fill with dry rice or lentils and bake in oven at 200°C to make a pre-baked shell. Allow to cool and fill with desired pie filling after removing foil, rice or lentils (of course).

Filling:

- Tinned apple or freshly stewed apple (cooled) or,

- Tinned apricots or freshly stewed apricots (cooled) or,

Optional: mixed spice, cinnamon, nutmeg, sugar and other fruit fillings.

Method:

1. Pre-heat oven to 200°C.

2. Roll out shortbread to line a pie dish 1cm thick — blind bake.

3. Place filling in pie and top pie with shortbread 1cm thick.

4. Brush with water and sprinkle top with sugar.

5. Place a small knife hole in top to let steam out,.

6. Bake at 200°C for 18–20 minutes or wait until golden brown.

7. Allow to cool or serve warm with cream, ice cream or custard.

Lemon Meringue Pie

The Lemon Meringue Pie is the famous one when you want to stick a pie in someone's face. It makes a mess of their suit, too.

Preparation time: 40 minutes

Baking time: 20 minutes

Oven temperature: 200°C

- Pre-heat oven at 200°C

- Prepare a half mix of shortbread from shortbread recipe (steps 1–4) for base of pie

- Roll shortbread out 1cm thick to line 23cm pie plate and blind bake base at 200°C for 12–15 minutes or until shortbread is light golden brown

Blind Bake:

Place a piece of tin foil in a pie dish on top of shortbread and fill with dry rice or lentils and bake in oven at 200°C to make a pre-baked shell.

Lemon Meringue Pie Fillings:

Group 1

Milk — $\frac{1}{2}$ cup

Cream — $\frac{1}{2}$ cup

Castor sugar — $\frac{1}{4}$ cup

Butter — $\frac{1}{4}$ cup

Group 2

Cornflour — $\frac{1}{3}$ cup

Milk — $\frac{1}{4}$ cup

Vanilla essence — 1 teaspoon

Group 3

Lemon juice — $\frac{1}{4}$ cup

Lemon spread/lemon butter — 350g jar

Method for fillings:

1. Place group 1 in saucepan on stove, melt the butter.

2. Bring to rolling boil.

3. Combine group 2 together in small bowl to a smooth paste.

4. Stir into group 1 until thickened.

5. Remove from heat immediately.

6. Place custard into cool bowl and mix in group 3 until smooth.

7. Pour pie filling into pre-cooked pie base.

8. Spread meringue topping on pie and bake at 230°C for 5–7 minutes until top of meringue is lightly browned.

Meringue topping:

3 egg whites @ 50g

$\frac{1}{2}$ cup of castor sugar

Method for topping:

Using electric mixer on high speed, beat egg whites adding 2 tablespoons of sugar at a time until all sugar is combined

Beat up to form a thick meringue.

Snickerdoodles

Nothing I say or do is original. I heard the word 'Snickerdoodles' at a trade show in Las Vegas and I wrote it down. Although I don't know anything about the American product called Snickerdoodles, I thought, "I like this name".

I got the word, then I had to put a product to it, so it's our own invention and it's a beauty. Again, it's a shortbread base with custard and fresh fruit on the top with glazed fruit. It's quite different.

Christine gave me the cold shoulder for two days because she thought the name was so ridiculous.

Preparation time: $\frac{1}{2}$ hour

Filling:

- Prepare half of Vanilla Slice Custard recipe following steps 4–6. Allow to cool.
- Fold 300 mls of whipped cream through custard

Base:

- Prepare shortbread from shortbread recipe from steps 2–4

Tom's Tip—I'm Not Going To Talk About...

I'm not going to talk about filo pastry because we don't do it. You can buy it at the supermarket and you can buy three-quarters pastry too.

Method:

1. Pre-heat oven at 200°C.
2. Roll shortbread 1cm thick.
3. Cut sizes to suit muffin tins.
4. Press shortbread disks into muffin tins to form cup shapes.
5. Pipe custard filling into shortbread cups.
6. Bake in oven at 200°C for 20 minutes or until shortbread turns into a golden colour. Allow to cool in tins.
7. Take out of tin and top with desired fruit, e.g. blueberry, raspberry or strawberries. Serve with cream or ice cream, how snicker-tastic!

Fruit Squares

Fruit Eccles, Blueberry Squares, Apple Squares, Apricot Squares, etc.

Fruit squares would not suit the traditionalists. At the Beechworth Bakery we do Australianised Eccles. And they're more Welsh than English.

Some people say, "Oh these aren't like the real Eccles", — but they're real Eccles at the Beechworth Bakery, because I bake the stuff that people want to buy.

We put in fresh apple, sultanas, currants and glazed cherries, whereas the original Eccles only have currants and sugar.

Like I said, everyone can adapt, and we did.

At home you can do anything you want: put in just apples and sultanas, or sultanas and currants without the apple.

We just put the glazed cherries in for that little bit of extra colour.

Every recipe is adaptable.

Tom's Tip—Tinned Apricot, Use the Juice

When you open your tin of apricot, if you drain the juice off, put it in a saucepan. Bring to rolling boil. Then add cornflour to thicken it up. You'll get apricot sauce.

Fruit Eccles/Fruit Strudel/Squares

Makes three large squares

Preparation time: 15 minutes

Baking time: 15–18 minutes

Oven temperature: 210°C

Ingredients:

Tinned pie apple — 1 x 425g can

Sultanas — $1/_2$ cup

Currants — 1 cup

Ready rolled puff pastry sheets — 3

Red or green cherries — glazed (chopped) — $1/_4$ cup

Method:

1. Pre-heat oven at 210°C.

2. Mix fruit together.

3. Place one cup of mixed fruit in centre of each pastry sheet.

4. Fold corners into centre and turn upside down on greased oven tray, Brush top with milk and prick with fork or 3–4 cuts with knife.

5. Bake in oven for 15–18 minutes at 210°C.

6. Serve hot or cold.

You can use any of the afore mentioned fruit — blueberry, apples, apricot, rhubarb, raspberries, or a combination of all (depending on what is in season) — to come up with your own special fruit squares. Here's an opportunity to start you own secret family recipe — how's that?

Croissants

Croissants are a pain in the bum to do. We do them in big batches, stick them in the freezer, pull them out, prove them, and cook a few dozen every day.

There is a lot of work in Croissants.

The best suggestion I could make about Croissants is to buy them from your baker; don't try to make them yourself. If it's too bloody hard, it's too bloody hard.

Christmas Pudding

Baking time: $3^1/_2$ to 4 hours

Ingredients:

Group 1

Raisins — $^3/_4$ cup

Sultanas — $^3/_4$ cup

Currants — $^3/_4$ cup

Flake almonds — $^1/_4$ cup

Rum/brandy/sherry — 3 tablespoons (one of choice)

Glycerine — 1 teaspoon

Group 2

Butter — $^2/_3$ cup

Sugar (brown) — $^1/_2$ cup

Vanilla essence — 1 teaspoon

Eggs — 2 x 50g

Zest of orange (fine grated)

Nutmeg — $^1/_2$ teaspoon

Mixed spice — $^1/_2$ teaspoon

Ginger — $^1/_2$ teaspoon

Plain flour — 3 tablespoons

Cake/biscuit crumbs — 1 cup

Method:

1. Combine all of group 1 and soak overnight in a bowl.

2. Mix all of group 2 to form a paste. Now blend together with group 1.

3. Place a large pot of hot water on stove top and bring to rolling boil.

4. Soak tea towel in cold water. Wring out so tea towel is still wet.

5. Lay tea towel out on table and sprinkle generously with plain flour, in a 40cm circle, and rub flour into wet tea towel.

6. Place mixture in a ball in the centre of tea towel.

7. Pull tea towel over mixture, tucking evenly and knot tightly with string, leaving just a little space for expansion. It's easier if you have someone to help do this.

8. Place pudding wrapped in tea towel into the boiling water making sure the water is kept at a slow boil with the lid on the pot.

9. Ensure the water does not boil over or run dry. Always add boiling water when topping up.

10. Cook for $3^1/_2$ to 4 hours.

11. When cooked, lift out and hang pudding to cool or it can be eaten immediately.

Serving suggestion:

Brandy Butter

Ingredients:

Butter — $^3/_4$ cup

Castor sugar — $^1/_2$ cup

Brandy — $^1/_4$ cup

Method:

1. Cream butter and sugar until light and fluffy.

2. Beat in brandy a little at a time.

3. May be covered and stored in refrigerator until ready for use.

recipe for success

This isn't just a recipe book! My recipes are based on my philosophy of life. The real secret of success is to be able to live the life you choose, and I choose to be a baker.

How can you start making something without knowing what you will end up with. So why not have a recipe for life?

Tom's Special

Here's a special recipe for you.

Preparation time: years and years and years

Oven temperature: as hot as you can stand

Makes: one good life

Ingredients:

- A bag of determination and a bloody huge bag of enthusiasm

- A diary or a notepad and a pen, for writing down your goals

- Pictures to help you visualise

- Uplifting reading matter and tapes

- Educational reading matter

- Chuck in an apple a day, because it's good for you

- Add not too much sugar, but plenty of spice, and away you go

Method:

1. **Clean up.** Clean up your kitchen; spring-clean your mind,

2. **Focus.** Remember that winners have two characteristics — definite goals and burning desires — so visualise what you are going to do next,

3. **Do it.** Mould, shape, create, chuck in the ingredients and bake it. This is your life!

4. **Enjoy your reward.** Stick all your hard work in the oven of life and enjoy your piece of the pie,

5. **Be grateful.** When it's all over, have an attitude of gratitude — and you'll not only enjoy your experiences as a cook, but you will also have a good life.

If you do all that, the happiness will follow. You'll be grateful to get up and go to work. (And there are lots of people in jobs today who are not happy about getting out of bed in the morning because they don't have an attitude of gratitude.)

It's having that gratitude that we're alive and living in Australia where we have some of the freshest food.

I've been to America, Europe, London many times, as well as other places, therefore I know that when we have fresh milk in Australia, it is fresh milk.

When we have fresh fruit, it is fresh.

And as for our steaks — I've been to Texas and Argentina, but I believe our meat is equal, if not better, than anything being offered anywhere in the world.

Australia is blessed with its array of fresh foods.

I'm especially grateful that I live in north-east Victoria.

It's a food bowl and the Murray River is a lifeline.

Clean Up Time

You will never get anywhere until you've cleaned up your act. If you want to achieve something in your kitchen — clean it up and your kitchen will deliver. Clean the benchtops, clean up the place. Get rid of the garbage. Spring-clean your mind.

You get upset with one of your in-laws,

> you get upset with one of your staff,

> > or you get upset with one of your co-workers.

> > > You carry it,

> > > > build on it.

> > > > > Next week you pick up some more garbage.

And you keep carting it around and it gets so heavy that you're weighed down — your back's hurting, your neck's hurting and you've got ulcers.

Keep Away From Gunnados

I like to visualise the product I've got to cook, and that's the same with life — I've got to see it. I've got to see it in my head before I can believe it. I've got to visualise the A-Model Ford car I want to drive around Australia again, I want to visualise that trip to Europe — that's how I start to believe that I can succeed.

So go to the travel agency, pick up the brochures, cut out the pictures of the Leaning Tower of Pisa or the Eiffel Tower, stick them on your wall and say "I want to go there two years' time in March". Keep visualising and saying, "What have I got to do to actualise those dreams?" If you want to get to Europe, the answer might be: "I've got to start saving some money."

It's the same in the kitchen; check out those pictures and keep saying, "This is the Apricot Pie that I want to make". You've got to see it in your mind. Get pro-active, don't be like those people who are always driving around looking for the town of Gunnado. They're gunnado this, they're gunnado that.

Most people don't do anything with their lives because of that fear of criticism.

I've never seen a statue made to a critic.

I've never seen a statue made to a committee either.

Them Goals

If you're serious about making a good product in the kitchen, read the books, prepare, set your goals, get that recipe. You should set little goals all the time, but you must set your bigger goals first. Most of us don't get serious. Most of us are talkers not doers. It's so easy to talk the talk, but to walk the talk — that's much more difficult. Get that fire in the belly and keep stoking it.

Most people don't set goals because they haven't taken responsibility for their lives. I never took responsibility for my life until I was 32.

Take responsibility for the product you want to achieve — and remember there's never only one answer to any problem. When I am studying a new recipe I will grab three to four books and then I take what I want and I leave the rest.

I used to think the goals were the start of success, but the start of success is taking responsibility for my life. It's not up to my mother, not up to my father; it's the choices you make, not the chances you take, that create your destiny. So choose to be happy.

Most people don't set goals because they tell themselves, "Gee, I couldn't make that beautiful cake, I'm not that good a cook". We put ourselves down with our false sense of unworthiness. Try talking yourself up instead. I've often got to tell myself, "You're okay, Tom, you're a good cook".

People don't realise the importance of goals. Most people just drift with the crowd and follow the followers. Most parents don't teach their kids to set goals. Most schools don't teach goal-setting. Most people only know about goals in sport. Most people don't ask themselves, "Where do I want to be in five years time?"

People say, "Tom, you're joking, why do I have to put it on paper?" The answer is that if you don't write down your goals, you'll set hopeless ones, like, "when I get home, I'll sit down and watch telly". Yeah, you'll achieve that goal, but that's not a great goal. And that's what most people do because they don't write them down. So their goal for the day is to get out of bed, go to work (where they don't want to be), come home, then sit in front of the idiot box. That's not a goal at all.

Goal-setting is the greatest form of self-motivation you could ever have. You write your own recipe for life, which no one else can do for you. Once you've done that, all you've got to do is adapt it to your beliefs.

If it's not on paper, it's not on this planet. If I don't have it on paper, I just keep changing the ingredients around and the recipe gets right out of whack because I'm not sure from where I started. And it's the same in life; if it's written down I can see where I'm getting off track and I can tell myself, "This is not where I wanted to go, this is not what I wanted to achieve". If you start off wanting to do a meatloaf and end up with a vegetarian dish, that's crazy. You think, "Oh gee, I didn't add the meat", but if you had something in writing, that wouldn't have happened. And just like in a kitchen, life is not always easy. All things are hard before they're easy, but one of the best ways to make them easy is to get them on paper.

You've got to have them goals wrote down.

And broke down.

You're got to have your goal written down, and broken down into bite sized chunks — prepare your onions, make your sauces, chill your eggs, find the sour cream and warm your oven, so you can get that beautiful product as your end result. You've got to achieve a lot of little goals before you can achieve your big goals.

I read some of my goals every day. Every day I read something positive in the first 15 minutes after waking up — before the other rubbish comes in. You become what you study, and if you want to be a success, study success.

I tick off points one by one as I achieve them. People might think I'm bloody mad, but I write out the recipes for my life for two and five years time, etc. People might say, 'Geez Tom, your life's pretty predictable'. Well it is — but there's a lot of spontaneity too, because if you've got the ingredients of success worked out you can do spontaneous things because you've got room in your life to go off and do them.

Just like in the scrolls or the pies, you can change the filling. You might set a goal that reads, 'I'm going on a trip to South America' but you can always add a bit more and say 'I'm going to California as well!' But if you don't really know you're going to South America, how can you add to it? It's the same with a recipe.

We've all got our dreams and hopes. Most people drift with the crowd, they follow the followers, who are going nowhere.

Utensils For Life

Life is just like a recipe for a cake. First you've got to know what you want to make, and after that, it's a matter of getting the preparation right before switching the oven on.

Tom's Tip—Assume: An 'Ass' Out Of 'U' & 'Me'

A lot of people assume they know what they are doing. Even though they haven't focused on anything, they say, 'Oh I know how to make that...' and then it doesn't really work out. Don't assume. (The word 'assume' means make an 'ass' out of 'u' and 'me'.) We assume we have that critical skill when often we don't, we've got to study and learn. I didn't really know how to set goals until I read about how to do it.

Preparation in the kitchen is just the same as preparing yourself for where you want to go in life: you've got to have the utensils. One of the main ones, I believe is positive self-talk — you've got to tell yourself 'I can add the improver to make the bread rise, just like I can improve my life and make that rise too'.

For me the utensils are audio tapes and the self-help books that I listen to and read. Fair dinkum. Then there's other stuff I would never waste time reading, watching or listening to because there's a lot of 'utensils' you don't need. Get rid of them. Some you'll never ever use, others you shouldn't use. They may look all shiny, but you don't need them.

But you do need knowledge: the more you learn, the more you earn. You become what you study. Now if you want to be a great architect, study great architecture. If you want to be a great mechanic, study cars. If you want to be a great artist — study the great artists. We all want to be great cooks, but how many of us bother to study it? If you want to be happy — study happiness. If you want to be wealthy, study wealth. Everything else comes down to self-discipline.

Boots 'n All

Enthusiasm is the elixir of life. Get in there boots 'n all. Nothing great has ever been achieved without that spark of enthusiasm. The believers pick up the prizes in life. So, get in there 100%, achieve and then move on. It's the same in the kitchen: get in there — achieve, and then move on to your next stage — into the dining room. And then later at night, into the bedroom — wow.

The average person gets out of bed in the morning, wanting to go back to bloody bed!

Who wants to be bloody average?

You've got to get out of bed in love with life and raring to go.

You've got to get excited.

You've got to be excited.

Fall in love with life.

If you want to be enthusiastic, act enthusiastic.

Honestly, we live in the best country on earth, we've got the best opportunities — we can even write our own recipe for life!

A lot of people haven't even got that freedom.

Oven Of Life

Finally you stick all the preparation I've been talking about into the oven of life. Then out it comes and you get your slice of the pie.

With recipes, I often make mistakes, but I believe if I'm not making mistakes I'm not really trying — mistakes are life.

I told the story in my book the Breadwinner about how I fell off my bike. But falling off my bike was part of learning — don't give up, just get back on that bike. Life is like riding a bike. If I don't use the bloody pedals I'm not going to get anywhere. It's like Thomas Edison said when someone pointed out that he had 5000 attempts before he developed the light bulb. He replied, 'I didn't fail 5000 times, I successfully identified 5000 ways it will not work'.

And this is it, if you keep trying something and it doesn't work, you don't need to go back there. But — that's the insanity of it all — most of us go back there, we do the same thing and expect a different result.

Today my recipe for life is achieving me heaps. I've got four wonderful kids. I lead a great life in country Victoria and I travel the world.

I live 'one day at a time' and I enjoy my life. It's a journey, not a destination. I've made baking my career and that been a real pilgrimage for me and I hope that you have found this recipe book helpful. I really believe in recipes, because once you've got the foundations right, you can add and add to them. But you've got to get those foundations right first, and mine haven't changed — I still am the boy from Tocumwal. I come home and my wife still tells me to take out the chook bucket.

I hope this recipe book helps people. Life is about liking yourself, liking the job you do and liking the stuff you make in your kitchen. Life doesn't have to be stressful, neither does cooking.

We live in this wonderful world.

Make a decision — whether it's right or wrong, make a bloody decision. Get out of your comfort zone and into it!

And when you've done all that, do that little bit extra. Because it's that little little teeny weeny little liddle liddle liddle liddle little liddle liddle liddle liddle little liddle liddle liddle little little liddle liddle liddle liddle little liddle liddle liddle liddle little liddle liddle liddle liddle little liddle liddle liddle liddle little liddle liddle liddle little liddle liddle liddle liddle little liddle liddle liddle little liddle liddle liddle liddle little liddle liddle liddle liddle little liddle liddle liddle liddle little liddle liddle liddle little liddle liddle liddle liddle little liddle liddle liddle liddle little liddle liddle liddle little liddle liddle liddle liddle little liddle liddle liddle liddle little liddle liddle liddle liddle little liddle liddle liddle little liddle liddle liddle liddle little liddle liddle liddle liddle little liddle liddle little liddle liddle liddle liddle bit extra that makes all the difference.

Tom's Tip—Have A Recipe

How can you start making something without knowing what you're going to end up with. So why not have a recipe for life?

The End

BEECHWORTH BAKERY
Australia's Greatest Bakery

BEECHWORTH

The Beechworth Bakery was established in 1984 in Beechworth and in September 2001 opened a second Bakery, the Beechworth Bakery Echuca.

Licensed to byo wine from 12 noon and open from 6 am to 7 pm daily for breakfast, lunches, snacks and early dinners.

Christmas mailing list available within Australia and selected products overseas.

If you can't visit the Beechworth Bakery today, the next best thing is to visit our website!

www.beechworthbakery.com

Beechworth Bakery

27 Camp Street, Beechworth 3747

Victoria, Australia

Telephone: +61 3 5728 1132

Fax: +61 3 5728 1455

Email: enquiries@beechworthbakery.com

Also by Tom O'Toole

Read about Tom's amazing life and
more recipes for success

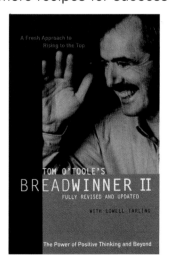

index

Notes